A Roof and Four Walls

URSULA BLOOM

A Roof and Four Walls

HUTCHINSON OF LONDON

HUTCHINSON & CO (*Publishers*) LTD
178–202 Great Portland Street, London W1

London Melbourne Sydney
Auckland Bombay Toronto
Johannesburg New York

First published 1967

*This book has been set in Fournier, printed in Great Britain
on Antique Wove paper by Anchor Press, and
bound by Wm. Brendon, both of Tiptree, Essex*

Men make houses, women make homes
Old Proverb

To
my good friend of years
TREVOR ALLEN

and a thank-you for everything
he has done for me

Foreword

Of necessity I have written of some of these houses before, and have on purpose skipped my experiences at the first house, the rectory at Whitchurch, well aware that they would be repetition, for which I apologise. I do not remember 'the little house where I was born', but the remainder are pieces of backcloth behind me: houses that have made me laugh or cry, with the deliciousness of change.

What influence has a house on a personality? Do I miss today the 'big house' of old times or are the passing houses better? Some have brought joy, some success, some a brightness which helped me, some brought tears.

Does my laughter still echo in fantasy through Hertford House in Saville Street at Walton-on-the-Naze? Do I still come down the lovely staircase as a bride? Do I still weep at 82 South Croxted Road, Dulwich? Or work hard and find success at Poona in the Harold Road at Frinton-on-Sea?

Do ghosts live? Do memories help or hinder? Does one leave something of oneself in a house, or could this be the light film of imagination? 'Nothing is ever lost,' said my mother, 'laughter and tears live on.'

How much lies behind an address, or how little?

Once my present husband and I picnicked on the lawn at Whitchurch, which was waiting for a new incumbent. It was a radiant day. Did I for a moment see a little girl dancing barefooted under the monkey tree as she did a long time ago?

Or is that ghost of myself still walking down the stairs at Harlow Old House? Or shutting the gate on Poona? Is there more attached to the house and its meaning than we know? Or is the address merely something on one's notepaper, something that one passes by, then goes on one's way and forgets? Is it a circle, and do we come back to the beginning?

URSULA BLOOM

Whitchurch Rectory
Stratford-on-Avon

This is the first address that I remember, in scarlet on my father's light grey notepaper, which I adored. Paper has always attracted me, but of course I was not allowed to use his paper, things like that were much too good for the children. There were two of us, myself and my brother Joscelyn.

I lived at Whitchurch until I was in my teens, and it was really a hamlet. Leaving Stratford on the Shipston road, you pass the turning to Clifford Chambers, the one to Atherstone, the next to Preston. You then meet that diabolically misleading signpost which says Wimpstone $\frac{3}{4}$ m., Admington $3\frac{1}{2}$ m., Ilmington $4\frac{1}{2}$ m.; Wimpstone is the parish of Whitchurch; the original village of Whitchurch is no more, save for the church, a cottage and a farm, but this is the postal address.

The rectory was important-looking, in red brick with a tiled roof. About it was the general air of prosperity considered to be so desirable in those days. It was urgent that one should maintain one's position, give the idea of riches even if starving, and generally comport oneself properly. We were equipped with massive coach-houses and stables, a dog kennel in which one could have kept a cow (two at a pinch), and our assets towards all this consisted of three bicycles. There were three acres of sprawling gardens, lawns (top and bottom, one for tennis, the other for croquet), and a capacious orchard of ancient apple trees. From this garden we lived on stodgy old apples, rhubarb and cabbages all the year round.

There were many bedrooms, drawing- and dining-rooms, my father's study, and no bath. That worried no one, for we were luckier than many in the neighbourhood, for we *had* got an indoor 'It', on the back landing, approached by a sort of ante-room so that it could be entirely private. All 'Its' were shrouded in mystery, bead curtains or something to give them that air. Nobody must ever know that you were there, for that was vulgar. The cistern did not fill up easily, so please-don't-pull-the-plug-too-often, a great problem when we had guests staying with us.

My father had his own 'outside place' for want of a better name; he preferred this; and the servants had an 'outside place' opposite the scullery door. We also had a filthy cesspool at the end of the orchard, and when the wind was in a certain direction, oh, my goodness!

You must understand that all this was the proper and desirable surrounding for a professional man. We lived there for years. We were always keenly aware of our insufficient income, the stipend was £300 a year, and also aware that whatever it cost we must give the bold exterior to the outside world. Prosperity was the flag we flew, and, believe me, under it all that flag was more than a little ragged.

We had innumerable friends, and in the early afternoons of winter a fire had to be lit in the damp drawing-room, in case somebody called. It would be almost indecent to be caught without a fire, yet there was the monumental problem that, if nobody came, the lighting of one would be a dead loss. And coal cost money.

Privately we lived in the dining-room, which was the family room. All dining-rooms had to be papered in red. They had stuff curtains in winter, chintz ones in summer, and all families spent their lives there, but nobody admitted this. The dining-room was slightly bourgeois, and we must be grand. We must do the right thing. All life was influenced by that infernal 'right thing'. If you dined out and they gave you game you had to provide game for the return invitation. If a children's party gave presents, then yours did the same. Talk about an army of copy cats!

We were the professional class, which was something, or anyway we thought it was. It would have been a gross indignity to be less. A 'shoppie', for instance. The most appalling thing in our lives would have been to be common!

When Queen Victoria came to the throne she produced the middle classes, which had never been here before. Until this slender, red-headed girl came to the stone of Scone there had been the rich and the poor. The 'poor' covered a fairly elastic group of people, such as shopkeepers, 'small men', and unprofessional ones, whose position in life did not encourage familiarity. One did not light the drawing-room fire for the 'small man'. The fire was only for the cultured classes, doctors, parsons, lawyers and such, with architects, dentists and vets hanging on to it, and always hoping that they would be accepted. The lady of the house usually put folk into their right niches and labelled them for the future. To say 'But he is not a gentleman' was the last straw.

All the same it was a thrill to live in a competitive era when everyone was trying to get to know the right people and lever themselves into that desirable position which was known as 'something better'.

I, being the child of 'class', was reared in a nursery by a stalwart nanny. There was a small gate outside the door, so that I could not possibly get out. My world was barred by that gate, and downstairs was the great big world of beyond where people did the most extraordinary things. Nanny was queen of my small country, and a tartar she was! Everything was done by the clock, and we were governed that way. The house was a red brick box which enclosed us, and as long as we lived in that sort of house we had to be that sort of person; what was more, we liked it.

But when I was seven Nanny left, and the nursery became

my bedroom, with a small downstairs room to use by day, known as the schoolroom, though nobody ever learnt a thing in it; Florence, the nurse-housemaid, took over from Nanny. Florence was not so stern, 'not the same class' was the way Nanny would have put it, for undoubtedly Nanny was more class-conscious than anyone else in the house.

Growing older, and sharing the dining-room for meals with parents, I heard all manner of projects debated. I was the only daughter, and marriage was very urgent for a girl, seeing that the future provided no other prospects for her. My paternal grandmother, an ambitious lady whose own sex life had been more than something of a problem for the scandalised family, wrote enquiring about my future:

> Is Whitchurch a suitable neighbourhood for darling little Ursula? Her future? I mean *men*? Any offers?

I wish I knew what the parental reply was.

The rectory possessed all those supreme comforts which today none of us have. Also, it was secure; inside its doors one could not imagine anything disastrous happening, and maids did everything for us. If a servant left, a queue immediately appeared at our back door beseeching to be engaged. Mother had no real worries. (Incidentally we had no landlord and paid no rent.)

We rose every morning in time for breakfast at eight. All had to attend this unless very unwell; no other excuse was per-missible. What a routine it was! At seven, when the hall clock struck, a maidservant arrived with a tin bath for me. She arranged this on a large mat in the centre of my icy-cold bedroom. She returned with towels, and a green can of boiling water ('And don't you get yourself scalded, miss'). Then she brought the ewer from the washstand (which was icy cold, too, and fre-quently had dead flies in it). All this arduous routine was gone through for a girl who was at the age when any thought of washing was singularly distasteful to her. When I got rid of the maid I poured out the water, setting the soap to float so as to give the impression that I had bathed in it. I then crumpled the towels, but stupidly left them dry, with the result that one of the more despicable of our housemaids gave me away. She told my father. He sent for me.

'Baths,' said he, 'are made to *get into*. Everybody washes, it is one of life's duties.'

I didn't understand it. How could such a sensible man have such scatter-brained ideas? He himself had an enormous bath like a huge tin saucer, and every morning he had a cold bath in it. In the time of a rime frost it made the whole household shudder; the way he splashed about making noises like a grampus, in fact he earned himself the nickname of Grampus from it.

We dressed, and this also was routine. Clothes had to be properly folded overnight, or pocket money suffered. Broken suspenders must not be safety-pinned as a last forlorn hope— (What is a needle and cotton for, dear?) A clean hankie was a vital necessity. No child wore jewels of any sort, or lace on the drawers save for parties. 'Why not?' I asked a favourite great-aunt. She was a modernist, and she beamed. 'Lace on the drawers leads to other things,' she told me. It seemed double Dutch to me.

As the gong was being rung for breakfast, and Fanny—the grandfather clock—struck the hour (all our clocks had Christian names), we trooped downstairs. How spruce it all looked! There were no agonies of getting it cooked. A leaping fire and a print-gowned maid both at the ready, the table itself and the side table covered with fresh white linen, initialled H.B. (all the best linen had to be initialled, that was a 'must'). When breakfast was over it would seem that none of us realised that we had not a thing more to do until dinner-time, called lunch by the best people. This was hard to remember, for when I was very small we did call it dinner, and lunch came into vogue to be annoying, I imagined. We must do the right thing, for it would be so awful to be common. What did we do next? It could be district-visiting, or going for a walk, or cycling into Stratford to do some shopping, or slipping out of the way. If it was summer I went off to the farm up the road, for a game in the farm-carts, with the chickens (once we let the ferrets loose, and that was *not* our morning!), or other little amusements.

In summer-time, when the lawns were in action, there were games we could play, but the unending demand of how to fill up the hours was always something of a nightmare, more especially when winter came. In summer we could fish for the family, or disappear. In winter we had to read certain books, all Dickens this winter, perhaps, all Thackeray next winter, or French exercises, or have a whack at learning German, or some other diversion which was never madly enthralling.

Breakfast was bacon and eggs almost always; we could not eat toast *and* butter *and* jam, that was extravagant! Lunch was meat and pud. Sunday's joint lived an unconscionable time in our house and went through all the usual ugly disguises. Sea pie. Hash. Mince. Curry. The lot! The rule was that nobody could be choosey; one must eat everything on the plate, and if one did not like fat, that was no excuse to get rid of it, or push it to one side. A dog was a useful member of the home in these circumstances, if he could be persuaded not to be noisy; a cat was convenient, if it was the right kind of cat, but some of them are highly selective, which was most distressing. One had to know one's cat.

Tea was *the* meal. Then one would not have thought that tea could ever be abolished, and the time would come when nobody had it, when the sacred hour passed by and nothing happened. Tea meant anchovy sandwiches, or Gentlemen's Relish for Dad, cucumber ditto in summer; bread and jam, plum cake, ginger cake, seed cake, pikelets in winter juicily buttered, and sometimes one of those rather vulgar little additions (not known to county families) like 'scratchings'[1] with brown bread and butter, or 'a faggot for your father who is very tired this afternoon'. There was dripping toast, and those *were* the days! Tea was the one unhurried meal when one could afford to be

1. Fried pork fat in rosemary.

leisurely, and then we talked. That was unless visitors had arrived, when we had that dreadful drawing-room kind of tea which my father disliked so much, cake-stand and all, and my great-aunt's special cosy with red roses on it in crochet.

Supper (when we were alone) was a dim meal of a patchy nature, and the day ended later with hot cocoa and cakes. But dinner was different. Everybody dressed for dinner; and the staff were in clean aprons, and newly ironed 'streamers' to the caps. I remember the first dinner I actually noticed, for I was very young, and I heard my father say to the boy, 'For heaven's sake go and clean up those buttons, you look awful!'

Oh, the rectory was comfortable in its own particular way, with nothing to do, and lots of time to do it in. Finances were our main agitation, for nobody must ever know about this, money was never mentioned, it was the most low-down thing there was, barring sex, and that of course was just too shocking! One had to have money, maybe sex was in the same category, but nobody discussed them.

The neighbourhood was busy with entertaining, and the Edwardian party was the best possible fun. I remember the trains to the ladies' long dresses, and the constant trouble I got into when walking behind them, and treading on them. I remember the children's parties, myself in white muslin, well starched and prim, with bows on the shoulders and sash to match. The bioscope was the latest thing to have, and considered to be a tremendous step forward into the future. Sometimes a conjuror was employed, or a man who wore a paper hat and sang songs to us, and we all laughed at the right moment. One arrived at the entertainment and there was a small gift for everyone. One left with hot soup to speed one on the way, and a cracker to take home for fun.

From the children's party proper one qualified (aided and abetted by time) for the boy-and-girl dance, which was a real delight. The mildly flirtatious came into the picture and were alarming, but intriguing, in one and the same breath. Suddenly

B

one realised that there was a great deal more to life than Nanny had thought, poor old duck! Florence was more knowing; she knew everything but wouldn't tell, was the conclusion at which I ultimately arrived.

The great effort of the adults was to keep the facts of life, and anything that was similarly rude, from the children. In truth my father did not hold with this. He was a man who had been born in 1860 with a 1960 mind, and he believed in the children knowing everything as soon as they were old enough to make enquiries. He was not assisted by the women in the roost. Nurses, governesses, and Mother all found truth too complicating.

'All those silly lies,' said my father, 'and they only mean you are landed into a lot of trouble sooner or later. You've got to tell the truth in the end, so why not start with it?'

'When they're older they won't ask such embarrassing questions, and never seem to mind who is there.'

'They'll always ask anything they want to know.'

Lessons were no worry on my behalf. No wise family wasted a stipend on teaching an eligible daughter, who would be sure to marry anyway. Teach-her-to-read-and-she'll-teach-herself-the-rest was the amiable assumption. That was the way I got it.

On the other hand my brother was despatched to a boarding school near Kidderminster, for he had to qualify for some position in this hard world, and the best positions had examinations as to what a lad knew. My father had dreamed of the Civil Service for his son, as he had shown open dissent to the Church. But there he was. The Civil Service maybe was not Joscelyn's future, even if he had liked the idea. It meant exams, swotting, and teaching others while at Cambridge in a desperate attempt to meet his fees, and perhaps it would *not* really suit him.

What about the British Museum, where my father did a lot of research work? Or the College of Heralds? He had a great many hopes, none of which materialised, and in the end he was forced to come to the conclusion that the future of a boy rests mostly with himself. He makes his own way.

Joscelyn went off to the boarding school, I contributing a bold half-crown to his spending money, and my income was threepence a week, save for the miserable bit I earned by typing for my father. At school Joscelyn learnt practically nothing, whilst I stayed at home at the rectory, and did exactly the same thing there. But anyway nobody was ever paid to teach me anything. I read, and I read, and I read, for in books lay my future.

Hundreds of people have been brought up this way in a square box of a rectory. Going out into the world later on, they have found, as I did, that the actual house had given them a sense of security and comfort, and a teaching of its own. Once, I remember, Professor Joad told me that country rectories gave a better training, and produced more brains, than any other form of home in England. That was the record. You may laugh at them, but they do something others cannot do. I explained that not a single penny had ever been spent on teaching me. 'But,' said he, 'you read.' Most rectories have good libraries, and plenty of time for this business of study. And where there is wide reading there cannot be a lack of education. And *was* my reading diversified!

The Book of the Dead engrossed me, the great novels, save Sir Walter Scott, whom I always detested. I had the *Daily Mail*, *The Times* and on Sunday the *News of the World*. A family of broad-minded sons at Alderminster—the next village—supplied me with a paper known as *The Pink 'Un*, to widen my information! Every day Harry Sharpe from W. H. Smith's brought our newspapers, and I had free access to his bag of magazines. We sometimes sat together and read them on the mossy banks of the lower lawn, quite contented, and not worrying about the unfortunates who were waiting for their papers and magazines.

The rector of Alderminster complained—with every right—and I thought that he was a beast.

One of the facts that helps most is that there are no strangers in rectories, everyone is a friend. One is so glad to meet people. The rectory in itself is there to help others, its whole system is to be of aid to the parish, and that is the greatest lesson of them all; what a help it is to be brought up in such! A red box, oh yes, it was all that; but inside it were human hearts, hardships and despairs; joys as well.

I was in touch with them all.

We had personal friends, of course, but people were fastidious about whom they could or could not know. The start to the century was dedicated to social routine. Can we know the So-and-so's? Wasn't the father a vet? If so . . .! What about the Smithsons? Isn't he a publican? You couldn't possibly let your women go to *his* house, not like that, could you? Ours were all received in the drawing-room (parlours were 'out'), and there the ladies discussed love affairs and local scandals *ad lib*. The neighbours supplied plenty of each.

Nobody enquired what the gentlemen talked about in the dining-room, though we were bursting to know, but they always laughed very loudly and sounded ribald. My mother used to warn young parlourmaids to keep away, in case they heard anything they shouldn't. If they did, it meant that the girl's mother came round and complained, almost blaming the family for it.

I don't think my mother need have worried too much, for the parlourmaids knew more than she thought, and after dark our kitchen and pantries concealed young shepherds and carters and such galore, and I am sure they chatted in much the same way as the gentlemen did. They were not supposed to be there, of course, though we never had any of the more stringent rules about 'followers' which some rectories had. My parents' principle was 'if they want them they'll get them anyway, whatever rules are made'. Also the place afforded the most excellent getaways if disturbed. There were ways out of most rooms, and young men caught unawares could scurry through the scullery door, and down the back garden at speed, or into the orchard, and hope not to have the bad luck to fall into the cesspool at the far end, but generally the awful smell warned them off in time.

I had discovered that if one behaved well in the drawing-room the guests were charmed with one's gracious manners, for it was the era of sweet little curtseys to the ladies and gentlemen, and 'ma'am' to nice old ladies, which is always telling. 'Be good in the drawing-room, and be yourself outside it,' Florence always suggested as being the happy way out of worries.

I had two boy friends, older than I was, who came in the summer as paying guests at the farm up the lane. I was forbidden to play with them, for they were considered to be 'common'. They came from a suburb of London, Woodford way, and their father was a commercial traveller. As I had a maternal uncle whose rôle in life was travelling in this and that, I argued that I thought it slightly odd to jib at it in others. I still think so. That argument got me nowhere, I must admit, so great were the intricacies and mysteries of Edwardian behaviour. I said this during lunch, I remember, and the maid who was waiting at table was hurriedly sent out of the room whilst we talked, in case I dropped another brick.

On the sly I met Bertie and Geoffrey.

The rectory being so lavish with its little byways and other ways out of a jam, it was asking too much to expect the chastity of a nunnery from a girl of fourteen. Florence gave me the idea. 'Why not have a little fun?' said Florence.

I went to bed at seven o'clock every night, because I was growing fast and needed long hours of rest. On hot summer nights this was far too early, for I could not get to sleep and got tired of lying there reading mythology, which was my passion of the moment. And if you ask me, you need only a little good mythology to give you all manner of ideas, what with Helen of Troy, the Trojan horse, and this and that!

So when the sun set and dusk came, I re-dressed and slipped out into the garden, with Florence keeping cave. Not the front garden, of course, for there the parents might be entertaining, with sloe gin under the elm trees, but we had plenty of back garden and several ways out of the place. I had sweet twilight assignations under the damson trees, in the farm orchard, up the road, or in the old barley barn (that was before the thing blew down in a gale), or in the dell, a secluded spot further up the lane; all this was far more engrossing than mythology. No, I did *not* take my brother with me! My brother was not very good at keeping a secret, and bribery with toffees (which was the only way I knew) was not entirely satisfactory, for he was one of those children who *would* talk. I went alone.

'You won't be wanting him,' said Florence, well aware of the private trouble.

I suspect that deep within me was the urge to free myself from the grown-up world, for I was singularly lonely. We could not afford big parties, and naturally people got sick of asking us out with such small or no return. But how enchanting to find companions here in the village! And what did I care if they were so-called 'common'? So whilst my parents and their guests chatted on the front lawn, believing me to be safely abed, I was in the dell dancing to imaginary music, with the lads whispering sweet nothings, and enjoying myself very much indeed.

But I had not reckoned on the fact that in this quiet hamlet, where everyone was longing for something to talk about, everybody watched everybody else. One evening when Geoffrey and I were talking earnestly enough, with arms about each other, suddenly it seemed that every bush had come to life, and I realised that we had an audience! Half the young male population of the place was busily watching us. We were playing Romeo and Juliet to a much amused audience.

I shrieked, and fled for home as fast as I could, for home was a hiding place, and I believed, as most young people do, that no evil could cross that step. Geoffrey had a fight with the nearest lad, and hurt him a lot, blacking both his eyes for him. It was more than irritating that this happened to be the top pupil in my Sunday School, the lad I really trusted. That taught me much.

I fled to Florence and sped up the back stairs which were presumed to be for servants only, and quite wrong for me; I stopped only when safely in my own room. Obviously romance was too exciting. It was too much of a good thing. One was safer with mythology at home; perhaps, after all, my parents had been right.

Had they found out?

They had not. Hearing something of a noise, they had attributed it to bat-fowlers, who were out and about at this time of year, and they never questioned what had happened.

It might not be so easy next time.

As the new century advanced, so did people's ways. Under Victoria, said my father, everything had been cut to pattern, and everybody had been good; one could not expect it to be the same under her son. He was not against the King; he had always thought that Edward VII had been brought up quite appallingly, and blamed Victoria and Albert for that. Mother, herself educated in Germany, disliked the German influence. Although the old Queen's morals had been excellent, they had neither of them really liked her, which was unusual for that period. Possibly the truth was that she had lived too long, poor old lady.

Now there were the difficulties which divorce was bringing to us. It was on the increase; even one's best friends, who should have been patterns of propriety to the village, went in for it, and it was deemed to be in the worst possible taste.

The Portmans had arrived at Goldicote House, he having been divorced by his first wife, and she having divorced her first husband. This upset the parish and because country people love gossip, everything was enlarged. Oh, how people talked!

Some said that Marie Corelli was privately married. Others that she had lived with her step-brother, Eric Mackay, who was an amorous man of many loves, as all the world knew. In fact when he died rather suddenly, and Miss Corelli went to the funeral, she was appalled by another lady's letters which she found lying about, telling her only too plainly what had been happening! She refused to go into mourning for him, just the sort of thing that she *would* do. Instead she ordered herself a white crêpe dress and wore that, for she adored being conspicuous.

The crêpe dress in white only increased the talk.

What was the real truth behind the charming Ellen Terry? She was the most lovely lady who ever came to the rectory, I thought, and she had a voice like a bell. But what about . . .? You know what I mean, said the neighbourhood, then, with the usual aggravating manner of grown-ups, 'Look out, that child is here.'

There was the enchanting Lady Warwick, who was quite the most beautiful woman I have ever met (with Gladys Cooper as a close runner-upper), and even I realised her loveliness. It was, said people, a trifle odd that the King came down (*incog.* of course), and everyone knew who it was he came to see. If there were visitors at the castle at the time when the secret code message arrived that H.M. was on his way, all of us had to vanish like smoke, and that went for Lord Warwick as well. The only way that one knew what was going on was by the presence of a policeman standing stonily alongside the port-cullis in the aimless manner of a policeman trying to be inconspicuous.

One day when we were lunching at the castle (I on condition that I behaved like a mouse) a man came round hawking baby elephants from door to door. Today the mere idea seems idiotic, and one cannot imagine that he got many buyers, but in the era of dancing bears in country lanes, hurdy-gurdys with monkeys everywhere, etc., all manner of surprising things did happen. Lady Warwick, mad on animals, bought the most charming little baby elephant.

'But what will you do with it when it grows up?' asked my father, who was rather dismayed.

She had not thought of that one.

The baby elephant trotted about after us rather like a big dog, but there came the time when if any of us got in his way he just put an adroit trunk round the waist, hoisted us easily enough, and popped us the other side of the hedge, which was a most humiliating experience.

There were visitors there all the time, also those rather frightening emus which Lady Warwick kept as pets, though pets was not the name I should have given them, for, goodness me, how savage they could be! I once saw a bishop in very real difficulty with them, his gaitered legs flying fast, and old mum emu coming along behind all fire and fury. One dared laugh at bishops in these days, for people were getting a little less smug, and the noticeable change in human behaviour became a worry to country parsons, who were supposed to abide by the book of the words. Probably we always felt that nothing really wrong could happen in a rectory, though where we got that idea I don't know, just as we were sure that ritual and faith would stand firm. The young have very great faith; unfortunately, as one finds later on, faith is not great enough.

I began to grow up.

I was now no longer eligible for the children's parties with bioscope or conjuror to start the ball rolling. I had had to abandon dolls, which was a real grief to me, and I was feeling that crackers were 'a bit young'. Now I went to the boy-and-girl dance, quite a different affair, given for young ladies in their teens with 'ankle skirts', and young gentlemen from their big schools, where they had learnt a great deal more than mere bookwork. Now there was no little gift beside your plate when you sat down to feed, but you did have a dance programme with a tiny pencil, like the grown-ups, and supper was served with a light hock, which always made me dizzy.

'You only have to get used to it. Top it up!' said a most fascinating young midshipman, who promptly pinched the whole bottle for us, and drank most of it himself.

Mother said that he was a dreadful young man, though she laughed. My father said that it was wise to remember that sailors were very fine fellows, and magnificent at sea, but when alone with the ladies one just had to be careful. Never trust a sailor, said my father. (I married one later on, perhaps because I have always adored men you could not trust.)

The whole of my life was changing very much. Although we are told that it was the coming of the first world war which changed everything, it had begun before that. The middle class was expanding. Naturally the right school and the 'Varsity were still vital to a young man, and equally naturally the middle class could not get these, for academics always wanted to know what the parents and grandparents had been, which was a bit of a jar to some. But it was the ambitious age, and now a maidservant sought to marry a shopkeeper and so keep a maid of her own. It was quite low down not to have a maid; that was a hallmark. The shopkeeper sought to squirm into the professional classes, and keep two maids, as a status symbol to the outside world. The doctor and solicitor kept a tweenie as well, and possibly a man to open the door for them, or a buttons. Everybody who was anybody had a boy to clean the boots and the knives, and usually to get the cook into trouble as well, but that little contribution was thrown in 'for free'.

It was a competitive world, which is always far more exciting to live in than one which is niched and pigeon-holed as it is today. The great prizes were within reach of everybody if only they stretched out far and fast enough. Oh, how very entertaining it all was! The fairy story still existed, and the beggar maid could marry a prince, if she was lucky enough to attract such a gentleman's attention.

The rectory was, of course, done up in a paper parcel, neatly tied up and sealed. It stood back from the road, one could not even get close to it from the lane. It was aloof and therefore dignified. It was safe, and even if we were poverty-stricken (and we were) nobody would have admitted it for the world. I adored the place, but I must admit that it had the hard side.

'Nothing awful ever happens here,' I told my mother, and one day to my horror I was disillusioned.

The darling old woman who took in our washing told me. I used to go down there and perch on a big linen basket in her back kitchen to discuss the affairs of state with her. I had always been taught that no one had ever been born in the rectory, nor had anyone died there. I was terrified of death, it had always alarmed me. Sometimes we seemed to be so very close to it in that village, but it had never come to my refuge, the rectory.

My parents had not encouraged this absurd alarm of mine. They were both interested in the supernatural, and possibly this was not really a help. They gave table-turning parties, Florence told me about them.

'That old tumbler goes whizzing around,' said Florence, 'and it spells out answers to what you ask it. It does really, and nobody knows who is pushing it.'

My people were interested in the occult, but did not think that it was a good idea for the young. I must admit that at that time it alarmed me.

One morning I went down to Mrs. Goddard's, and perched myself there as usual. The steamy atmosphere of the place fascinated me, we could hardly see each other in it, and she and her daughter caught the most shocking colds through it. It was she who told me about the rectory.

Somebody *had* died there, and, greater horror still, actually in my bedroom! Could anything be worse? I listened in misery to this, searching for more knowledge, yet hating to hear what she said when she spoke. It had been the son of old Mr. Pritchard, the first rector to live there; he had had five children, and the daughter of the house, the only one, had eloped with someone who was supposed to be 'not quite nice', whatever that may mean. She had driven away with her love, the sexton had seen her. But the youngest son had died of that menace of the Victorian era which was known as 'the decline'.

'But no, he couldn't have done!' I gasped, round-eyed with horror.

'Oh yes, miss, he did! I know he did, and he died in *your* bedroom,' said she.

How awful! was my first thought.

I went home in an agony with the idea of immediately changing my bedroom and taking on the spare room, which was a nasty cold room facing due north; it had mice in it as well. Nobody worried themselves too much for the guests who stayed in it, because we always felt that out of common decency they could not possibly complain.

I was not allowed to change my room.

My parents explained that I had slept there for many years, and had been completely happy there, so what was the trouble now? I had seen or heard nothing, and I never should, for the spirit of the poor young man was somewhere else. I had a crucifix hanging by my bed, and that should be sufficient. Did I doubt Christ? No, no, of course not! Leastways not very much, I added to myself, but I was *not* too happy about it.

A box of nightlights bought by Florence helped a lot. 'Don't you worry, dear,' said she affectionately, 'it's just a lot of rubbitch. I know that in my room one night a young blacksmith got a ladder and climbed up to it, and got in and did you-know-what-I-mean to the maid who slept there, but that doesn't worry me. I don't pay no attention to that sort of thing.'

Darling, darling Florence. What a sweet thing she was!

I owe much to the rectory. It guided me through childhood to the beginning of the teens, and then on into them. But trouble began.

My father was a man born with a flirtatious nature, and he was very much attracted by an 'affair' and later found difficulty in extricating himself. He played with fire, and *we* got burnt. The hour came when I had to learn that there is no front door that you can shut on the world, and no blinds can be pulled down on sorrow, for it comes just the same.

The atmosphere of the rectory became one of bickering, constant scenes, my father's absence on genealogical work, and my mother fretting at home. To every child the division of parents can only be a wretched problem, which hurts more than anything else, for the ground is kicked away from beneath him. I had never thought that my parents would separate (that, I felt, was outside all limits of possibility), but they did. My mother tried to stay on; she hoped that when my father had time to cool down from his latest attachment he would be sorry and want things as they had been. She felt that if we went away for a time and he found how miserable life was without us, then he would be sensible.

We went into rooms at Stratford-on-Avon. In November, Whitchurch was shockingly damp and depressing, we caught constant colds, and the children were always ill. All this was used as an excuse. What we did not realise was that the world was still Victorian at heart, and clergy and their wives do not part. The clergyman could do no wrong, he *must* be in the right because he was a good man, had to be, to be a clergyman at all. This was the idea. Therefore the fault must lie with the wife, even if she had the children with her. We had only a pittance to live on, and always the nightmare horror that if the news got round of what had happened, and the Bishop started to enquire too closely, my father would lose the living, after which nobody would have anything at all.

It came as a tremendous blow to me when I saw that the rectory in which I had been brought up was no longer safe. The gate of security was swinging away from me. I was terribly young, very little way into the teens, yet in some strange manner all those teens were snatched away from me, and taken completely away. I grew up. Someone had to help my mother who was shattered by events, someone had to steer her round this very dark corner, and there was nobody save myself. The curious thing was that years later, when I became a widow, I recaptured those lost teens in a house called Poona—and that name was no recommendation for a house. I lived through them again. It sounds quite impossible, and something of a dream, but it is true.

The hired carriage came for us, and my mother and I went out and got into it. All hired carriages smelt odiously of moth-balls, and my brother (who at this time was absent at school) had always said that they smelt of caterpillars too. Musty. Of another world. We drove away. I sat there with my pug dog Romeo clasped in my arms, trying hard not to cry, because that could only make it worse for my mother. There was the sound of the horse hoofs clopping, and we left it all behind. The gate of the first home I had ever known closed behind me.

41 Shottery Road
Stratford-on-Avon

The boarding house was not really what we wanted, and even if we thought of it as being a haven for a time, it grated. Mother and I had been through too much. I know that I felt estranged, as though I had left part of me behind in the rectory, and this was a new self living here in the small town, to which I was not used. I had indeed left something behind me, it was the joyous happiness and independence of my teens. I had grown up. It happened in but a few minutes, perhaps when we turned the corner of the lane into the high road beyond. And the high road was my life.

Public opinion was against us. It was not the thing for people to part company. If the rich could do it, the poor could *not*. And as a clergyman could do no wrong, Mother had undoubtedly been 'up to no good'. That is life, especially in small towns. Some people cut us, and we could do nothing about it; others were patronising, and we could do nothing about that either.

We had a tiny sitting-room to ourselves, which was pleasant, and across the road lived a doctor and his wife who did not get on with each other. They quarrelled when eating, and their dining-room was opposite our windows. When they got really worked up they threw the cheese plates at each other, providing a constant source of entertainment for us. I have never forgotten the joy we felt and how we laughed when she made a bad shot with her plate and brought down the gas bracket.

After a very sticky Christmas, spring came, thank God, and Stratford began to get itself prepared for the Shakespeare Festival, which they took in a big way. This was the time of year when everyone hoped to make a fortune, so the boarding house put up its prices, and that was very much that. Rooms are not easy to find in Stratford when the Festival has got the town in its clutches. We knew this, but finally we found digs in the Shottery Road, which was more off the beaten track. It was in a dreary row of workmen's cottages leading to the top of the hill. Everything was to pattern, variance lay only in the curtains, and the washing on the back clothes lines. I hated it, but we had to get somewhere, and it must be where we could afford.

There were a policeman and his wife next door to the digs and they told me of number 41, which would shortly be to let. It was ten shillings a week (four beds, front and back room, outside kitchen and 'It', and a strip of garden with the railway at the end. I thought that would be nice to set the clocks by).

I was hungry for a roof and four walls; I wanted them quite desperately, believing that all homes *were* homes. They are not, and I was soon to find that out. We took the cottage, and when the summer came we moved in. That, of course, was a ghastly mistake.

On one side of us were the policeman and his wife; they were dears. On the other side was the young man who propelled Marie Corelli's gondola up and down the Avon. Miss Corelli (who pretended to hate publicity in any shape or form) had done the unusual thing of buying a gondola, brought down to her with an Italian gondolier (the real thing) who had taught the young Englishman next door how to work it. But whenever Miss Corelli went out in it she had trouble. Photographers appeared. In the end she took with her a rug behind which she and her companion Miss Vyver hid, if needs be. Both of them were such large ladies that they ought to have appreciated the fact that no rug could ever completely conceal them, and some people got the most amusing snapshots.

The gondolier was an amiable young man, but I had to admit

that nobody seemed particularly pleased to have us at number 41, and a little later on they made it quite clear that they positively disliked us.

We did everything dead wrong.

We had no line of washing hanging out on a Monday morning. It seemed that they judged character by the washing. We had a 'woman in' to clean down every day, and this was snobbism. We had friends to tea, quite unknown for the road, and not to be encouraged. Once I called to Mother to follow me out and bring the gloves I had left in the drawing-room. I did not know that 'front room' was the right name for it. After that people called 'drawing-room' after me. I felt rather sick inside. Frustrated. I did not know what to do next.

We kept all the wrong hours. We got up later in the day than other people did, for we had nobody to see off to work. We stayed up later, too, and some evenings had friends in. I had never thought that practising the piano was noisy or ostentatious, until one night when a brick-end came through the window, considerably scaring me and my pug dog. We had to face it out. There was no line of retreat, and if there had been we should not have taken it.

When people visited us we quaked lest windows would shoot up and rude remarks be hurled as they waited on the step for us to open the door. It was so much worse when visitors were affected by it.

What was so trying was that I was one of those girls who stay pretty in their teens, and I was attracting male interest. Not that I cared too much for men. There had been enough trouble with my father at the rectory, so that I felt slightly scared about love.

The road gave me a bad name, as anyone would imagine, and frankly I did not know what to do. It was the era when cars were just coming into their own, and young gentlemen looked Mother up (though I don't suppose they really wanted to see her) and left their cars outside the door. Once a neighbour put a three-inch nail into a back tyre for the young man. What happened? They found that it takes more than a three-inch nail to put off an ardent young man!

I had thought that home was one's own, and that it had privacy. It was somewhere where one loved, wept if one wished, or laughed if one felt that way. But I wasn't laughing very much in 41.

They detested me because I swam daily. I was a very keen swimmer, practising for racing and interested in life-saving. It was an era when women did not go in for athletics (save for the occasional egg-and-spoon race), and the fact that I swam and rowed infuriated the neighbours. 'You only go there after the men,' they called after me.

It was quite untrue. I was swimming when only women were there, and you don't meet men sculling an outrigger on the long reaches and trying to improve your timing. I never even *saw* a man there.

All this was doing something to me, for I was afraid inside. I had got to put a brave exterior on it, for that was the habit of the generation from which I came, but all the time I was panicking, for I was far too young to cope with it. That was if anyone ever could have coped with it, for there did not seem to be a way out.

The landlord, who was a Methodistical man, joined the ranks of defiant neighbours, and this was a shocker. He had found that my father was high church. 'Goes about in a woman's skirt,' was the way he put it. Privately I was rather distressed over that, until my father burst out laughing and said, 'They all think that; laugh it off. What does it matter, anyway?'

The policeman next door was goodness itself, and oh, how he helped me! He wanted Mother to take some action, but we were most reluctant to do this lest it added to the trouble. It would have been better if my father had visited us more often, nobody was ever rude to *him*, for he was a large man who faced up to a foe, and had no rot about it. We dared not face up in case we made it worse. It was like playing cowboys and Indians, and ourselves being the cowboys and losing all the time.

c

On his own the policeman passed a warning down the road for us. He told me one day when I was in there that he had done it, and for fun I had tried on a pair of handcuffs.

'Now that's got you, miss,' said he.

It hadn't got me at all; by some extraordinary trick of my own, I was out of them. 'There we are!' said I. 'Yah boo!'

His face was a miracle. He said, 'Well, I'm blowed!' then again, 'I'm just blowed!' and finally, 'Don't you ever go in for shop-lifting, miss, or we shall have a job with you when we get you!'

He had found that our Methodistical landlord had a nasty little habit of wandering up the Shottery Road at dusk. Then, if he was taken that way, he had a sly peep through our letter-box. We had not known this; the policeman—being a policeman— had. One night he waited for him in the small alleyway between our house and that of the gondolier. When the landlord appeared and trotted up our two steps to pry through the letter-box the policeman put out a staunch hand and grabbed him by the shoulder.

'This is trespass, sir,' said he.

The landlord did not do it again, but it gave us a rather wretched sense of doubt as to what would happen next. I had the feeling of someone watching us all the time, of someone waiting to pick me up and set me down with a bounce. For the first time in my life I was afraid of my fellows in the world, and this was not good.

'This cottage is doing something to me,' said I to my mother. She too knew that, but what could we do? We had a lease and could not pay up and get out. We had to go on. Maybe one of the biggest mistakes we ever made was going on with 41.

Frank Benson wanted me to join his company. He got me round to his dressing-room in the old Memorial Theatre, and had a talk with me. I sat on a props basket, that was all there was for the visitor, and I shuddered with fear. Goodness only knew that 41 had made me much more scared of people. I said that I wanted to be a writer, and he made me recite Juliet's farewell to him. Then he suggested that I went on to the stage. I said that I could not leave my mother.

'But she isn't ill. Why can't you leave her, you silly little girl?' he asked, and gave me a talking-to. 'Your mother is your dad's job, not yours.'

At that moment I could hardly admit that my dad was not being particularly good at his job. I wonder what would have happened if I had taken that turning off the high road of my life? Too shy, I thought. Too much worried about other things, was more like it, without a doubt.

That autumn the horror began, for Mother had an operation which we hoped was for mastitis, but which we found was malignant. I knew that she would recover this time, but there was possibly another time ahead, the eternal menace of that trouble. I was too young to know all I did about grief, but working in a parish teaches one the harshness of truth in no measured terms. The rectory had done that for me. It seemed as if everything was coming at once. The moment she was better she had to get away, and we went to stay with her uncle who lived in St. Albans.

My mother was one of four (her mother had been one of three)—Uncle Arthur, who toyed with the law (not entirely flourishingly), my grandmamma, who was four-foot-eleven of proper little pest, if you ask me, and Uncle Jacob. As a boy he had suffered from osteomyelitis and was told that he would never live to grow up, so was boarded out on a farm at St. Albans really to die. He died there in the nineties, some time later on.

Heath Farm still stands on the Sandridge Road; it had comfortable rooms, warmth, good food, and oh joy, a bath with real taps! Uncle was a dear to me; he thought I had had too hard a time and needed fun. There was a dance at the Town Hall, and he made his eldest son, who was forty-ish, take me to it, for he said I needed a change. He even contributed to my dress for it. He was quite the nicest great-uncle to have.

Of course, you know what happened! 'And what the devil did you expect?' asked Uncle, when Mother argued.

It was the dance of that era, with Archibald Joyce's band, and the foxtrot (very new); naturally I met *the* young man. Montie was twenty-two, very much older than I was, an architect who earned £120 a year, which at that time looked like a fortune to me.

Until I went to that dance I was a silly child. I budded that night! Flowers everywhere, delicious music, the kitchen lancers (far more my line of country than the foxtrot), and the two-step. When ultimately my cousin got me away in the carriage, he longing to get home, he said, 'It's remarkable to me that the young man isn't still with us.'

Heart throb had begun, and in a big way.

When I got home we wrote to each other; he was interested in my writing and had given me a writing book as a present, which went straight to my heart. He came down to Stratford for Easter, which was the season when the river opened up, and there was the earnest scrape for the money to get the subscription for the boat club. I must say that he did *not* like the cottage.

'Houses influence people more than they know,' he said; 'it's like some sort of backcloth, and in time you become part of that backcloth; this one is wrong for you.'

At the time I didn't think that he knew, but he did. He hated all those gaping neighbours who muttered rude remarks, so did I, but what could one do? Mother would have agreed if she had liked him, but she did not like him, and that was that. My father came over to meet him, he was more tolerant, but still thought he was not exactly 'me'. The family had hoped for a rich marriage; don't blame them, they had suffered too much from poverty, so that maybe they realised that there was something in a stout banking account and very little in £120 a year.

Arguments began, but all these were swept under that summer, for my brother left school. He came away with few honours, he had not liked it very much, which was usual in those days, and he had not a clue as to what he wanted to be. I got out the bike and went over to Whitchurch to see my father about this. He was in a bad mood. Whenever you have to discuss some down-to-earth project in this world this is what happens. He said that he had paid the school fees, and he considered that he had done his bit.

We had a row and I said everything that I was ashamed of, but I was in such a state of flurry and worry, and how in the world should I break this news to Mother? Somebody had got to do something about it, and home I pedalled.

Acting on the advice of others I managed to get the aid of one of the Guinnesses, who then lived at Ettington Park. He introduced my brother to a bank in London. It was my idea of deadly dullness (his also, of course), but for the moment it would be an income of £40 a year, and surely that was something? A whole £10 a quarter looked like bliss to me. He was appointed to a branch in West Hampstead, and went off to digs in that neighbourhood. This was a dreadfully expensive arrangement.

This was when Montie came forward. By now he and I had one of those secret engagements which are always so popular in the teens. Nobody was supposed to know. I had a tiny dress ring, we met whenever we could, and that could never be often enough. He was all for our leaving Stratford. We went up the river in a punt and got down to a solid discussion. Number 41 was doing nobody any real good, it would be far better to move towards West Hampstead and have Joscelyn as a lodger. It would be at least more economical.

The man is a genius, thought I, wallowing in the superb joy of being half in love. The only thing to do was to talk Mother round, always the problem of the teens.

Montie was a great help in dealing with the landlord, for he knew all the tricks, and he managed to get him to waive the rest of the lease. This was a move in the right direction, and Mother was so pleased that we had boiled eggs for tea, which was something of an occasion.

'It will be such a joy to leave this place,' I said in the dining-

room which looked across a paved yard to the coal-house, with
'It' the other side. It was not the best view in the world, and the
noise the trains made at the far end of the garden deafened us
at times. The old joy of putting the clocks right by them had
begun to get a bit stale.

Montie suggested that we went to St. Albans, because we had
Uncle there, which would be a good start, and because it was
handy for West Hampstead. He knew most of the likely houses
and could get us one, at least in a better surrounding than this.
As far as I was concerned no surrounding could be worse. Life
had not improved since we came. Our original idea of holding
the head high and gallantly sailing past rude behaviour had not
worked out. They still called insulting remarks after us, and we
had no defence against them.

Montie was proving to be a big help. Mother was grateful,
but not so sure of Montie. She had not wanted me to become
what she called 'involved' so young. She had better ideas for
my future, for Mother had all sorts of maternal hopes, but she
did trust Montie about the house, and that summer he went back
and got us one for the September-to-be. It seems absurd that
neither of us saw the house first, but we didn't. We thought that
he knew. Rent was the major importance; it was £28 a year,
rates £5. It had four bedrooms, the same as 41, three sitting-
rooms, a conservatory and a nice garden.

At last we shall have a home again, I thought, for 41 had
never been this. Everything that was awful had happened there.
My mother's illness and operation, and for ever the dark fear
hanging over us like a curtain. My own loss of youth and being
hurled into the problem of ways and means, of trying to sort
out a difficult situation, and the hope of my father coming round
being in the end banished for ever.

'Don't fret for this place,' Montie said on his last visit, when
he and I stuck a sack of hay up the front-room chimney (I had
now learnt to call it the front room), so that when the next
tenant lit a fire, what ho!

That delighted us.

My last night there I could not sleep, but lay awake staring out across the orchards which then covered the other side of the road, towards Bordon Hill. I wanted to get away. I just hated this, and somehow I knew now that one could not hate a place without it reacting on oneself, and badly. It would be nice to be at Heath Farm tomorrow, and stay there till we could move in, in about a week's time. Very nice to see Uncle and Aunt again. But I felt old. Perhaps I *was* old.

It would be lovely to start all over again, and Montie had assured me that in the new house the neighbours would not worry me, quite probably I should not even know them. At this hour I rather wanted to step out into that friendless world of suburbia, anything to escape the nosey parkers of the world which I was leaving.

What I did not realise in that hour was that I took the scars with me. They are always inescapable.

Thornlea, Hatfield Road
St. Albans, Herts.

It still stands there, and it has still got 'Thornlea' carved into the gable. The first thing we noticed about it was that a rowan tree was fruiting in the garden, and it looked bright. It was semi-detached, for it was at the tail end of a row of small houses, with Granville Road running up beside it. We went up the steps to the front door, and entered a small hall with stairs rising ahead of us. At 41 we had had what was known as a box staircase, which was enclosed and entered by a door, significant of the cottages of about 1892.

There were drawing-room, small study, and a quite large dining-room with a little kitchen opening from it, and into all these rooms the sun streamed radiantly. Upstairs three beds and a bath. I did not realise that no water was turned on to it, for that is the way a bathroom can have you. You accept it on its face value, and it had no face value really, for it was purely ornamental.

This house accepted people. Mother immediately noticed that the 'dweller on the threshold' was amiable, which we took to be a good omen. It had been newly papered and painted for us, and had that nice smell of new paint everywhere. In the garden the hollyhocks were still flowering, which impressed us, and both of us agreed that Thornlea was a very different story.

But, of course, what neither of us realised in that hour,

perhaps because it was so entirely foreign to our own world, was that this house conformed to a pattern of living, which the rectory had never done. Here were people who worked in the City. At eight-thirty every morning each house emptied itself of its male population, and the women were left to drool through the day as best they could. At six at night the roads were swarming as a flock of bees—the city workers—returned to roost. The only difference between them all was that some of the women ran to the gate to welcome them, or came halfway up the street. Others did not care. One day as I passed a newly opened door I heard the most unwelcoming female voice bawl out, 'Oh I suppose it's *you* again?'

They would leave us alone to live our own lives, which was what we asked; I never even knew the names of the people next door, and hardly ever saw them. But how should we fill our days? What did we do here? No friends, and the farm quite a distance off. No visitors, for we knew nobody.

The wretched part was that now, leaving our immediate neighbourhood, it became plain to people (and this went for Heath Farm too) that my parents had separated, and this was not 'the thing'. Marriage was for ever, nobody who was decent did this sort of thing. So although Uncle was always a darling, we found that constant visits to and from the Heath were not encouraged. This was aggravated by the fact that the milkman cooked our bills (he would not admit it), and we got landed with payment for a dozen eggs we had not had, and the excuse of 'it being in the family' did not quite cover it. Mother went up to Heath Farm and had this out. I don't think the beastly eggs were worth it, but she felt that this was an injustice, and we had too many injustices to bear.

If I had thought to find my youth again I was wrong. Those teens, gallivanting, frolicking and gay, have gone for ever, I said to myself. Now I'd be old till I died, and I did not want to be old. What next?

On the Saturday when we had got the furniture in, and the

place really did look very nice, my brother arrived carrying a pot of white heather which he had bought as a gift to celebrate our moving in. The first thing he said when he got me alone was that he did not like the bank.

'Now don't you start that one!' I warned him.

He came down to the truth. The bank did not like him either, he said, and this was, of course, dangerous. If we had just moved here to be near him it seemed awful that he was in one of those sticky positions which would not work out. He had been there on three months' probation. It was a funny thing that nobody had noticed this before; now we went more closely into it. They would not be wanting him after the three months were up. I gulped hard.

'A fat lot of use the white heather is if that is what it does to us!' I said.

In another six weeks he would be here with us for good, and what would happen then? What indeed?

Mother suggested that I wrote words for songs, for the ballad had come into its own, and to my amazement some of my lyrics were accepted. I published several of them, but this brought in nothing more than a dribble of shillings, half a guinea was good payment, and even in those days half a guinea did not go that far. I wanted to write, read wildly everything I could, and got nowhere. There was plainly some time-table, some method, which I did not know, and I was missing my target all the time. What was it that I did wrong? I must say that Montie was undaunted in his efforts to find out.

But now, with Joscelyn back on our hands, what could we do? 'It's quite obvious that I have got to earn something,' I said.

Nothing could have worried my mother more. She felt that it would be derogatory. Her era had been the one of ladies' companions and nursery governesses, and she could think of nothing else for me. It was detestable for her. Maybe, poor darling, she had harboured the idea of my marrying a duke. She

did not know then that had I done so, my middle years and old
age would have been spent in showing horrible crowds round
the ancestral home until my legs nearly dropped off me, and
nobody would have the decency to tip me, because I was a
duchess! I should have been overworked in life and embalmed
in death. Not my idea of something cosy!

I thought of nursery governessing with very small children
(I did not know sufficient for older ones), and the most I could
hope to get was £20 a year, which was hardly a living wage.
Fate dropped the plum into my lap. There are moments when
fate works for you, and maybe the dweller on the threshold gets
sorry for you, or something similar happens.

Montie's firm was designing a cinema and putting it up at
Harpenden; they were approaching opening day. The owner,
who had a German wife (later she became a bit of a pest when
the war arrived on us, and the whole world went madly anti-
German), was searching for a pianist. The pay was thirty
shillings a week, which looked like a fortune to me. I would
play every night from five-thirty till eleven, and he wanted
three matinée days a week.

'Those matinées will never pay, he'll drop them to two when
they have been open a fortnight,' Montie prophesied.

Neither of us thought that Mother would be particularly
pleased. When I suggested that I went to a cookery class I had
heard of (I had sufficient money over from a birthday to pay the
very modest fees) she had blown right up. I liked cooking, and
if I qualified perhaps I could earn good money at parties. Mother
felt that to be just 'cap and apron' work. Today I wish I had
done it, for the hour did come when all the cooking descended
on me, and I could have done with greater knowledge of
it.

Behind Mother's back, I know, I went to Harpenden and
introduced myself to the cinema owner. I did not like him very
much, he had glittering black eyes, and a handlebar moustache,
in black also. But I knew he was stuck for someone, and he more
or less had to engage me. He closely examined all my certificates,

appeared to think nothing of them, and then asked if Montie could speak for me. I said that I thought he could.

Cycling home along that very dreary road, I got a puncture in the loneliest spot, and I had a very formidable afternoon. Ahead lay the awful prospect of breaking the news to Mother! I arrived back when she and my brother were in the deepest slough of despond. He had gone off to the Sphere Arc Lamps for a job, and had been taken on as an apprentice. *There was no pay.* For three solid years his family would have to support him, as Mother pointed out to him. He seemed a trifle dazed. I went round next day and interviewed the manager myself, but all he said was that I ought to be thankful that he had not asked *me* to pay for my brother being taught! 'That,' said I frankly, 'would have been absolutely impossible.'

The row over the Sphere Arc Lamps cooled down after tea, and he went off to air the dog in Clarence Park, and then, of course, I had to tell Mother what I had been doing this afternoon, only mine was *with* pay.

She was quite wonderful over it. She went very quiet at first, I should have expected this, then she said that perhaps she could help me. The season ticket to Harpenden was cheap, we could both have one, and on matinée days she could come in and help me, for she played beautifully.

I suppose at that hour it never occurred to me that already, as Montie had said about houses, Thornlea had started to mould me. I should join the stream of workers. I should catch a certain train and come back by a similar one. Do houses gradually sneak you into a certain way of living because that is the only way of living *they* know?

'Could be,' said Mother; 'we know so little about the things which really matter in life, of course, too little.'

That was when my brother returned with the dog, who had had an imperial fight, and, as usual with pug dogs, had got the worst of it, choosing a terrier as his foe! We washed and bound up the dog, who was not pleased with us for doing this, and then my mother said, 'You don't know what Ursula has done!'

as the beginning of telling my brother what had happened. He showed not the slightest interest.

The cinema opened with a tremendous gala night, and I had never realised that hands could ache so much, or hours be so long. How I prayed for *God Save the King*! At first the piano was set on the balcony, but it caught the echo from the roof, and sounded vile, so I was moved down behind orchestra curtains, in the front row of the fourpennies. They were supposed to have no idea who sat on the other side of those fusty curtains, but the gentlemen (I really must congratulate gentlemen for an enormous capacity to discover where real fun lies) found that I was there, even in the complete darkness. They proffered bars of Fry's chocolate cream over the curtain railing. They pinched any protuberance which offered itself, once it was the wrong part of my mother, and that was the day when the feathers flew! Naturally it was my fault. It always is.

Every Saturday night when I was worn to a frazzle I got my thirty bob, threepence off for a stamp. It was a fortune. Mother had ten of it, the rest was completely mine. Oh joy!

'You won't go far on that,' said the owner one day, but never made the delightful suggestion that it could be more.

'I shall get far enough,' I told him.

Perhaps the worst part of all was waiting at Harpenden station winter and summer till the midnight train came in for St. Albans. Montie and I waited there rather than at the cinema 'in case people talked'. One had to be very careful in case people talked. That was unthinkable. When the train arrived, into it we got, and out again at St. Albans, saying good night to the engine driver whom we got to know, and then we walked home to Thornlea.

I went straight to bed, too tired for supper, so I never got any, just a thermos of Ovaltine left by the bed for me. I slept till ten next day. It seemed dreadfully lazy, but what else could I do?

It was like starting life all over again. Grown up. Maybe I'd grown up at fifteen. Maybe it didn't really matter.

Thornlea was comfortable; there were no worrying neighbours, no worry at all save that we were not happy there. We knew no one. We hardly ever got asked to Heath Farm, and were not aware of our neighbours' names. I don't think I have ever felt such loneliness before or again, even in Whitchurch where you could see for miles, and if you saw a cow you were lucky. On Sunday nights, the only night when I was free from the cinema, I used to go out in the twilight to look into the uncurtained windows of other houses. With envy. With hunger, in a way. I wonder how many people there are in the world who are hungry for friends.

Mother and Montie did not get on well together, and there were constant arguments. She was right, of course, but, like so many people in the right, she set about it the wrong way. The fact that anyone was 'against' him fired me to hang on. My brother progressed at the Sphere Arcs, but alas not as far as earning money, and we were still very much on the rocks.

The cinema held on fast. But the dark smokiness of the air began to tell; at times my eyes seemed to be strained from constant looking up at the screen and being so close to it. I had a hurried lunch at twelve at home, then on matinée days caught the train to Harpenden, after which I never got another meal until I arrived home to Ovaltine at night. I lost weight. My bright colour had gone, and I turned deadly pale; this is the way I have stayed for the rest of my life. Once I had a flush that was like my rosy father, but that had gone, never to return. The sense of joyous liveliness went with it.

'It's anaemia,' people said, 'lots of girls get it.'

I thought that this would go on for ever. Bickerings about Montie, arguments *with* Montie, the eternal grind at the cinema, though I loved the people I worked with. Lovering, the operator, who was a darling, and who once bought me an ice-cream. 'You just ought to have something in your life,' was the way he put it, and how right he was! Miss Rogers, gaily vivacious, and such fun. The pay-box girl, Miss Chatton, who was 'ever so refined', but could count, which I always envied. The chocolate boy, who was a dear.

I caught my train and came home again. I was part of the machine of this part of St. Albans, for we had found that we were not living in St. Albans proper. The moment one crossed the railway bridge one got out of the dignified part of the city, where 'nice' people could live, and came into the part where the common people dwelt. *Nobody called on the common people.*

'I suppose there always has to be something,' said Mother with much regret.

This, I told myself, is going on for life.

In life nothing goes on for ever, even if it looks exactly as if it would. One happy July day, a Sunday, we all cycled over to Hertford and Hertingfordbury for a picnic. We walked in the woods there. Mother and Dad had been married at Hertford, so we made something of an occasion of it, and it was one of those heavenly days which stick fast in the memory.

My brother nearly caught a squirrel, quite by mistake, of course, and it was exciting. He then rounded a corner of a sudden, and disturbed a pair of lovers; the young man rose in a fury and said he would fight Joscelyn. Mother and I rushed to his rescue, and the young man left us using some words that I had never heard before. We had doughnuts, the sort of pre-war doughnut which had no relationship to today's brand. We went to the girls' Bluecoat School, and we fell in with the most attractive little Japanese lady selling something odd in the gutter. It was two pieces of cardboard clipped together; you opened them and turned the two pieces (which looked like wide stalks) over, and they opened up into three coloured balls of tissue paper, pink, yellow and blue. Each time they made a different pattern, they really were most fascinating (one penny). Everybody purchased some of the little Japanese lady's wares, but how she ever got there I don't know.

We came home in the half-light, and next morning the newspapers had the first sniff of the coming war.

'This,' said Mother with horror, 'is going to stop all that,' and she indicated the window open on to the road beyond our house, and the city workers starting for the City in their hordes.

'But how could it?'

'How couldn't it!' she said.

I rushed up to the music shop in Chequers Street where I went weekly to hire music for the cinema, and I got all the European national anthems that I could. When we opened with the Pathé Gazette it was to see warships steaming off to unknown destinations (*Rule Britannia* with a vengeance, and loud cheering from the fourpennies!). Little did I know that in one of them went my second husband as a midshipman.

After the thrill of war—and oh, how we wanted it!—our big picture with the world's sweetheart coquetting, went a bit flat: *Hearts and Flowers*, *If I could plant a tiny seed of love*, and *I'll be your sweetheart*, but cutting no ice at all. Montie pushed his head round the curtains.

'Have you got the Belgian national anthem, for there is something about it in the nine o'clock news?'

'I've got it,' I said.

It was one of the evenings when a gentleman who played the cornet came in to perform with us, and was an infernal nuisance, slipping out for a quick one, and not returning soon enough. The management said I ought not to let him go, but what could I do? Tonight the house was excited with the idea of war. Thrilling rumours were going round everywhere; love was very second on the menu.

That night, when we walked to the station in the dark, Montie told me that already things were changing. Brooker, our commissionaire, was on the reserve, and had got his calling-up papers. He would have gone by tomorrow night. They were having a whip-round for him, and the owner had not given a bob. 'A bit mean, I do think,' said Montie.

Things did move fast.

Next day the riding school behind Heath Farm was taken over, and quite a lot of men were already joining up in case they missed any of the fun. Joscelyn was one of the first. Two days

later the black flow of city workers was smaller, almost unbelievably so. One could not have foreseen that the pattern of
living would change so soon.

'I've joined up,' said Montie three days later. 'I have got a
week to settle things here, then off I go. Destination unknown.
Of course, it can't be for long. We all know that.'

Somehow one was too thrilled to be horrified, only glad to
be alive in such exciting times. Exalted. In his spare moments
Montie had managed the cinema, and now it was impossible to
get anyone else. The owner came down some nights, but knew
little about the real working, so that I had to check the trays and
the box-office money and plan billing ahead. I was far too young,
but there was nobody else. I only hoped they would not find out
that I could not count.

'Anyway, you're a most reliable child,' the owner said, and
it was the only nice thing that he said about me. Alas, I let him
down. I was playing the piano, scratching out war news on
smoked slides, arranging future programmes, and totting up
this and that. In addition I was keeping idiotic hours. I got
scared of the dark walk to Harpenden station last thing, sitting
there for an hour and arriving about twelve-thirty at St. Albans,
then walking alone up the steps and over the bridge on into the
Granville Road.

The pattern of living was changing and I felt that I could not
keep pace. I had constant headaches, I kept fainting for no
apparent reason, and was getting stupidly nervy.

'You're crocking up,' said the very nice Scots doctor. 'You
ought to live by the sea, that is the air you need.'

He had a theory that with generations in the north of Norfolk
I was starved for something which I did not get here. He
thought that the cinema was sheer slave-driving, even if my
mother did help me. I needed the sea, he said, and then, 'This
sort of life is no use to you, catching a train to work, and a train
back, and what a time of night that is to catch a train!'

We talked it over.

Could it be that I did not conform to the suburban routine?

D

I had come here and thought that it was quite lovely after that awful cottage in the Shottery Road; now was the routine engulfing me? Swamping me? Actually threatening me? I had never thought that midnight at Harpenden was a silly time of night to be catching a train, but of course it was.

Mother and I discussed this. The sea was an idea. Now, with the fear of the war getting worse, houses were going for a song on the east coast, so the newspapers said. Everyone expected that sooner or later we should be bombarded, or even invaded. The older people, the die-hards of the time, maintained that if Napoleon could not do it, why did we think that Kaiser Bill could? (We asked the same question when Hitler was there.) We had with mid-October given up the idea of winning the war by Christmas, for the first casualty lists had been a jar, but all the same we were supremely confident that in the end we should be all right.

The sea had the pleasant prospect of offering an income, and we *did* need that! We could let rooms, or take in boarders, or something of that sort, and the war was bound to be over by next summer, we said.

Mother went off to the east coast to see what she could do about it, and she came back joyfully, for she had actually taken a house at Walton-on-the-Naze. She had gone to Walton to see a house called The Moorings, on the Naze, but when she got there she learnt that some of the high tides came across the road, and one could have to take to a boat. That was not Mother's idea of fun. Coming back into the town, she happened to see a notice TO LET in Saville Street and turned up it.

'It almost seemed to beckon to me in the sunshine,' she said.

There was a little old Father Christmas of a builder who coaxed her inside, and I expect her old pal the dweller on the threshold influenced her a bit; she took it at £30 a year and the rates were a fiver. Those were the days, God bless them.

I had a farewell night at the cinema, though nobody sent round the hat on *my* behalf, and the owner did not even thank me. He thought it just too bad that I was going. I walked up to the station alone in the thick heavy darkness of autumn in wartime, and I waited there wondering what this new venture would bring about. I was dead tired. It seemed awful that I should never see any of them again; I never did, save years later when Lovering heard me in a broadcast and rang me up. I went to see him, and oh, how lovely it was to see such a dear old friend!

We sub-let Thornlea for the rest of the lease to a couple who did not like the bathing arrangements. We had not liked them too much either. They got the water put on in some way, and said they had a special heating apparatus which they left with us to be installed. 'For,' said the lady, 'my husband would *die* without a bath.' My supposition was that he did die, for the first thing the furniture removers unpacked when we got to Walton was the heating apparatus, and that should have been the end of the husband.

Had Thornlea done something to me? Yes, in its own way. I had stepped into a quite different rut, and the rut had made me really ill. I could hardly believe that I should never again look at a clock and say to myself, 'Heavens, it is still two hours to *God Save the King*!'

We were off to the sea.

Hertford House
Walton-on-the-Naze, Essex

I was enchanted by Walton.

We got there in the pitch dark, our journey and our apprehensions added to by three goldfish in a bowl, one pug dog on a string, another in my arms, and a kitten in a basket. I must say the black-out did Walton proud.

'We shall never make it,' I said to Mother.

Black as pitch, silent as the grave, and no one about. We groped out way down into the little town. In those days they had no adequate railing along the cliff, but trusted to a bit of tamarisk and one's common sense. How we did not plunge down to our doom, heaven only knows.

We went into rooms two doors from the house which was going to be our own, and after breakfast next morning I saw Hertford House for the first time. It was 15 Saville Street then, re-named by me after Mother's wedding town and the happy day we had spent there just before the war, and meeting the little Japanese lady who sold such an enchanting toy.

Hertford House was old, with delicately rounded bay windows and a fanlight over the door. It was far more than a roof and four walls. I had always wanted to have a fanlight. Once a mansion, it was split in two, but even then we had eight bedrooms. This should be good for business when visitors returned to the east coast to celebrate the ending of the war.

The leisurely hall reminded me of Whitchurch, and the shallow stairs had a sort of oriel window behind them. There were three bedrooms on the first floor, mine looked out over the Backwater, and what a vista that was, especially for a girl who adored mud!

My husband always thinks that I am mad about mud, but to me it is so beautiful, so tender, and so colourful with the sunset on it, almost like a dream. 'The poor child gets taken that way at times,' he explains.

The second storey had more bedrooms and bathroom, but here my cup was full, for it had only the outward and visible signs and no inward and spiritual grace at all. It had only ice-cold water. It seemed to me then that there was a jinx on us, we'd never get a home with a bathroom which really worked. There was another bedroom out of the dining-room, and over the kitchen.

'You like the house?' Mother asked me rather anxiously.

I adored it. It was an experienced house. It was kind and lenient in its influences, it had known dignified living and nice people, and I felt it.

We stayed a week in digs, and got the furniture almost arranged before we went in, and had engaged a maid. One could engage maids in those days, very good ones. That first night when I went up to bed I felt the house almost saying to me: *One day you will come down these stairs to leave for ever. . . . You will marry from here. . . .*

Hertford House was so gentle and old, and it almost seemed that it could talk. I lay awake listening to the noise the sea made, and the spray touched our front windows, for then there were no houses on the corner space, it was just wild land, tide-touched at times. Lying there I thought about houses. Maybe I had needed the unhappiness of 41 to teach me about life, and the hard work of Thornlea to teach me about effort; now I had come here, and there were still lessons to learn. Hertford House came exactly at the right moment. Montie had joined up and gone, the love affair with him. Now we knew that my father would never want us back, and perhaps to know for certain was almost a relief. We were starting all over again.

It was hard going for those first few days, even with a little maid to help, but we got all the curtains up, and the rooms tidied (or almost), and the place looking pleasant.

The old-time spirit of the days when Walton was a fashionable spa had, of course, died, but there were still lovely houses there, the marks of other days. The Albion was at the end of the road, not pretty, and round the corner the Marine Hotel with dear old Mr. Barker there. He would sit by the front door on sunny mornings, reading the paper, and with his dog. He was so kind to me, but the Barkers are kind people, and that tie has held fast through the years. In the summer-time there were teas on the lawn with maids in caps and aprons, and the hotel had a quiet old-world dignity which was enchanting.

Early on the lifeboat went out, and I rushed to see it. It was terrifying, how would they ever survive? Walton is a working sea, not just a place where you paddle. There were firm sands at low tide, and how beautiful to take the dogs along them! But at the period of time that we had chosen to live there, there were many noises-off out at sea. Talk about things that go bump in the night! And they were worrying.

Then out of the blue the previous torment returned. Mother suddenly had to have another operation. The house was hardly in order, but something had to be done immediately. Those were the days when one had an operation on the kitchen table, moved into one's bedroom for the job. My father came down. Nobody had expected he would, but I met his train at that very dark station, and we walked down to Saville Street together.

'What a place this is!' said he.

We got back to supper which had been prepared in the new home, now almost settled, and mercifully he liked it. He was not optimistic about Mother, and I was in no mood for discouragement. He said that all along he had known that the trouble would return. I had had hope. One feels that God is good, and why not now? Then my father changed his tune and started to talk with far greater interest about Walton. Apparently there were some special fossils up on the Naze, which could be found nowhere else in England, and he was off there first thing in the morning.

I know that I cried myself to sleep. One would have thought that later on I should associate Hertford House with bad luck and unhappiness, but that never happened. The house and I loved each other. It was gracious, and in a way did something for me in that it gave me a new poise, which 41 and Thornlea had rather taken from me.

The local ladies called. We went out to tea parties with hot buttered toast and cakes; then the cakes became nastier with the war, and the hot buttered toast less juicy. These were not the years for good food. There was Nick (Mr. Nicholson) the solicitor and his wife; he was a very kind man, not understood there, and sympathetic; she was rather odd, I doubt if anyone ever *knew* Mrs. Nick; there was the vicar and his wife (her pet name was 'Cold Toast', so you know what she was like!), and he was bearded, not the friendly type, I felt.

The Essex Cyclists arrived; now it seems absurd that there could have been a cycling regiment, but there was. This meant entertainments, parties, dances and concerts, which were just the thing for a girl of my age, and life was opening up for me.

I was a great help when playing the piano in soldiers' clubs, and accompanying. I was quite an attraction at dances. Even if the war was quite awful, and these days we had a menu of broken biscuits because they were cheap, and the oddest cuts of meat (when we could get them), life was still thrilling.

When summer came I could bathe. There were bathing machines along the beach (that was before huts came to beaches) and in the bathing machine one was drawn out into the water by a lean old horse which was then unhitched, and he came back for one twenty minutes later. It was thought to be highly dangerous to bathe for longer than twenty minutes. I swam twice a day, and hoped to take this on into the winter; I got as far as November one year and thought I was doing fine, then I got a good old head cold. No, said my mother in no measured tones. The bother is that once one breaks the routine one cannot go back to it, so I never did.

When the Essex Cyclists departed, just as we had come to know them all and were enjoying ourselves, the 24th London (The Queens) arrived. We did not get billeted in Hertford House, though the money would have been very useful, for they did not put men where women lived alone.

'One day the war *must* end,' I said.

At that moment the most almighty bang came from out at sea. 'It doesn't sound like it,' said Mother, quite composed, for nothing ever shook her.

'I wonder why they have to do that sort of thing here,' I murmured when I could speak again.

The Queens entertained gaily. We had fake landings and went out on one nose-skinning day in February to watch the practice. The Queens' men waited in sandbagged trenches, and destroyers came scuttling out of Harwich. They came before they were expected, which was the first blow, and something was wrong with the first shell (supposed to be a blank) which they sent over, for the whole trench at the Pole Barn Lane end of the cliffs quietly slipped down into the sea. The destroyer had the neatest ideas, I thought; it was the first time I had ever seen anything like this. She fired, whizzed round so that she offered her tail-end only as a target (I don't suppose she called it that, but it looked like it to me); then when one thought all was quiet she spun round again and sent a second shot in.

Something went very wrong! The Army had been quite sure that their part in the exercise was going to be a wild success, but it was a dismal flop. They hoisted a white flag to stop the firing, but nobody seemed to see it. An army captain, whom Mother had thought was a charmer, made some remark about where had they got their eyes, which did not impress Mother at all, and left me a bit mystified. We crossed him off our visiting list.

I knew the subs and the young captains, and amongst them were Anito del Riego (Teresa's brother, and a dear) and Arthur

Denham-Cookes, and other most charming men. I had come into my own. The gracious house was used to girls who wanted life, and I went out to dances, to concerts, to parties and to gaiety. Goodness me, how I needed it!

My mother's illness was getting worrying. She was having radium treatment every six weeks at the Radium Institute in London, and if ever there was a pull on our income, that was it. We stayed in a women's boarding house in Gower Street, 19s. 6d. a week for cubicle room, breakfast and high tea. You can imagine what it was like! But I was getting better, my colour was a little restored, I had put on some weight, and looked more myself, and I made clothes rather well, so had come into my own.

At Walton it was the Army. In Gower Street, University College Hospital, which is a teaching hospital, quite early in my visits there woke up to the fact that there was an attractive girl in the neighbourhood. My mother, deeply worried for all the anxiety I had suffered, was all for my having a gay time. I was the age for it, even if I had skipped my teens in some miraculous way of my own. I must confess that I rather liked last-year medical students.

'Only be careful,' said Mother, 'those young gentlemen know too much.'

Years later, when I had an op at that hospital, my charming little nurse said to me, 'We have such nice quiet students here, never any trouble with them,' and did not know why I laughed.

Mine were the days when one defended Phineas with the life blood, and other hospitals tried to invade and take him away. Those were the war years, the bad years, but the mad years in other ways. And mad years matter to a young girl. Mother was amused, but always worried lest I got hurt. That is the menace with all parents.

The new summer came to Walton, 1916, and a warm and lovely year it was, but the war was going badly. My brother was serving out in Egypt, which put him out of danger's way, which was one relief. But Mother was getting worse, and often was beset by the horror that she would never see him again. We were living with a ghost at Hertford House, not the ghost on the first landing, who never did anything worrying, but the ghost of the illness slowly killing my mother.

She was desperately anxious for my future, for I should have nothing, and at this time Arthur Denham-Cookes came to the house. He was rich, in the early twenties, with a big car which he drove madly, and Mother liked him. He was shy, musically-minded, and the Victorian musical evening had not quite died out. We had happy times round the piano, and maybe that began the story which was to end in disaster. Arthur always said that Hertford House was his second home, and that he adored Mother. He wished that he could marry her, and that was, of course, the road to my heart.

I gathered that his family were eccentric in the extreme. His strange mother wished to be an invalid, and his sister seemed oddly undeveloped in various ways. The two of them had had a father who was in the seventies when they were born. Their mother was herself out of touch with life, and tried to conduct her marriage on 1880 principles. Prudishly brought-up, it would have given her a fit had they known anything rude, whereas all my life *was* rude. Rectories are like that.

Arthur loved old houses, and originally came to see us because of the house, because of the good-looking daughter too, I imagine. He tried to say it was because he was interested in Queen Anne architecture. One of the subs remarked that it would be a damned sight nearer the truth if he admitted that he liked young women. That was how it worked out.

We became engaged in the first heat-wave of May 1916. That afternoon the world changed, and I could feel it. The house knew it in some curious way of its own, and when Mother said, 'Arthur is coming to supper, and he wants to have a talk with you,' somehow I knew that a door was shutting on the past and opening on a new future. The atmosphere told me, for atmospheres can talk.

We had that talk in the front room, today I called all front rooms 'front rooms', and could not stop myself. I'd never have a drawing-room again, I thought. That was where I was dead wrong. Arthur and I had our talk and he went up to the Albion to bring back some champagne, and suddenly Mother and I did not know what to say to each other, for everything had altered.

'I am so thankful, just so thankful,' was what she said when she could speak.

There was, of course, going to be the terror of meeting his rather odd mother, still living in Number 6 Prince's Gate, which then was a mansion, but today (1965) is a stumpy little house dwarfed by the big flats around it. We felt that the war would be over by this Christmas, we'd get married in the early autumn just about in time for the armistice. In the middle of all this Mother had to have another operation, suddenly out of the blue; it meant that things were bad with her.

Her condition was worrying, more so in that Arthur never thought that she was as ill as his own mother, and *his* mother had nothing at all the matter with her. She wanted me to visit her. One ghastly day Mother and I went along. In agony we rang the bell, I quaking lest I had come in the wrong hat! The butler opened the door to us with aristocratic elegance. 'Madam is not receiving this afternoon,' he said coldly, and shut the door again.

I was furious.

I returned to Walton and had my first—not my last—real row with Arthur. He behaved extraordinarily. He whipped out a Colt, much to my alarm, then leapt into the Sunbeam saying that he was now going to London to shoot his mother. He then went.

'He must be mad!' I told Mother.

'Nonsense, he's only acting,' she said. 'Let him go and have a row with his mother if he wishes; he'll never do anything dreadful really, it is just that he has the Irish impetuosity.'

Maybe she thought that.

Back he came next day, quite cool, and sat down on the big sofa. 'I told her what I thought of her,' said he. 'She's deaf, you know, but I damn' well made her hear. She'll see you on Wednesday.'

That was when I rose. 'She won't,' I replied. 'Mother is not well enough to do that journey twice, and you can tell her so. Now bring out your Colt and shoot me!'

I think he realised that maybe he had taken the wrong angle, for he sulked a while, then started to be more sensible. He'd get her to write and apologise. In the end he did not exactly do that, shall we say he got her to write!

At no time did it strike me that Arthur was ill. We had several peculiar scenes when out came a revolver and for a moment the world shuddered, but he quietened down. Perhaps the Irish are made that way.

In August the regiment moved to Frinton and all arrangements for the wedding were changed. 'Conky'—pet name for the C.O.—wished the ceremony to be in Frinton. The old church was the tiniest place, very very sweet with Burne-Jones windows. Then there would be a hotel reception, which would ease the work.

Mother and I had made the trousseau together, keeping this dark, because we had already found that the Denham-Cookes did not take that sort of thing at all well. Presents galore poured into Hertford House. I knew I should hate parting with it, but we should have to give it up, for Mother could not stay on there alone. She was moving into a small hotel in Frinton to be near me, and this could easily be her last winter. One hardly dared think of it.

Arthur had planned to go on living in his billet, which was very small. I wanted a home and a background. He was a man of moods, for suddenly before November the 14th he decided that, after all, he wanted a furnished house. The C.O. had said that digs were idiotic. Good for Conky! thought I. I must get down to it now, immediately, said he, and find him a large furnished house that was not too expensive; tonight. Quickly, said he.

I got out the old bicycle known as the F.S. (Family Steed)

and pedalled along the cliff path to Frinton. In those days this was possible, for the earth cliffs had not slithered down into the sea in the way they did later. South Lodge stood almost inland, with a road before it, and a wide cliff verge beyond that. Today it has all gone. Then poor old Pole Barn Lane had a promontory, with pond and trees, and now that has gone. There are about two miserable trees left, and even the Lido, which Nick got going there one summer, went into the sea with the rest of it.

But what a rough ride it was along that path on a bike! What an ear-biting, red-nosed ride it was!

I had never thought that it would be easy to get a house at a moment's notice, and the first one the agent took me to see I disliked very strongly indeed. I felt it had spooks there. The next one was a fairy-tale house, it was the dream-come-true type of house. It was ostentatious. It had everything. We had been so poor, adhering to cold mutton and bread, without butter, and 'this is not the day for pickles', that I had somehow never thought of the joys of money. I was used to cheap and nasty houses like 41 and Thornlea. Now Thalassa.

It was, of course, the most luxurious home that I shall ever have. Quite the grandest, and I was intensely proud of it, yet that house did absolutely nothing at all for me. It had no personality, it was just a roof and four walls.

It was situated on the Esplanade with the Queen's Hotel on one side of it and the house called Yarra on the other. Both Thalassa and Yarra are down today, and in their place are some of the usual modern flats. Poor Frinton! Once the snobs' paradise, the heaven of the east coast, what has happened to it now?

In the soft twilight of a dying autumn day I entered the glassed porch and went on into the gracious lounge-hall. There was the drawing-room, beyond it the study, and the large dining-room where fourteen or fifteen could sit down to eat. Beyond those windows, the garden with the grass tennis court. It was beautifully furnished. There were ten bedrooms, and the super bathroom which caught my eye. Also the hot-water system did work. In fact everything worked in Thalassa.

My eyes danced as I went to the big windows and saw the sea stretching before me. 'Thalassa' means 'the sea,' I thought suddenly, though where I got that from I don't know, seeing that I cannot speak a single word of Greek.

But then I always know the oddest things. A man once told me that when I was not four years old he watched me sitting talking to my dolls on the lawn at Whitchurch. Coming nearer, he realised that I was reciting poetry, but not the nursery rhymes that he expected.

'Arms and the man I sing,' said I, 'who once by fate and haughty Juno's unrelenting hate . . .' then stopped dead.

I nervously asked about the rent for Thalassa and the agent was most helpful. Apparently it would, if unlet next week, be in the hands of the licentious soldiery, so that the owner would accept almost anything. Would Madam care to make an offer? Madam was something of a little minx, for she offered thirty bob a week!

Madam got it!

I bicycled back to Walton, taking the road this time, for the cliff path could be dangerous in twilight and I was in a daze of joy. Getting married was fun! Arthur brought Mother along in the car immediately. He would love the position, I knew. Indeed he did, because the Queen's Hotel was next door, and they had an excellent bar. All of which goes to show that men and women see things with quite different eyes, for I had never even realised that there was a bar there.

He thought we needed more than one bathroom. He and I had been brought up with dissimilar standards, and I had never been class-conscious, it isn't the right line in rectories. He had.

He had been born at Number 6 Prince's Gate, and the third footman had told the butler, and the butler had reported the joyful news to his antique father, so he told me.

'Sir, you have a son.'

He said this with a good deal of pomp, and I being a guileless girl imagined that he was pulling my leg. So I went on with the story for him. 'And your father said "How's Madam?" ' It was a pity I said it, for it was most unpopular.

He and Mother stood in the dining-room of Thalassa, with that very thick carpet on the floor, and the pictures of wild animals on the walls. I noticed the one of the black puma with the vivid green eyes.

'Do they really have those things somewhere?' I asked.

'I'll take you to the wilds to see for yourself when the war is over,' he promised me.

'God forbid, if they do have them there!'

So I took Thalassa. I remember that on my first day there I had seven baths in all, and nobody else got a single drop of hot water, for we ran out. The cook, Mrs. Bunthorpe, said quite fiercely, 'Madam likes bathing?' It was the first chance I ever got to bath as much as I wished, and oh, how I wished! In the end I settled for three a day, and those were always quite the best moments of my life.

Leaving Hertford House made me sad in a way, but now I found that it had perhaps been a resting place in life, a time when I could re-establish myself, and not character-forming. It had not done anything like that for me, it had just been sweet.

I had come here on an icy November day with a nor'-easter blowing, and the echo of guns at sea. I had seen my first enemy aircraft here, big clumsy Zepps zooming round, and the whole of the Harwich peninsula apparently on fire. I was terrified, but my mother was excited beyond belief, for she never knew fear, and said that this was better even than the opera, for you did not have to pay for your seats!

I was going away. I was getting married. Hertford House had said that on the day I first went up those stairs. *One day you will come down these stairs to leave it for ever. . . . You will marry from here. . . .*

The Denham-Cookes insisted on a lady's maid, for all their ladies had them. I must say she was certainly not wanted by the Blooms, but she appeared on the scenes. She disturbed me a lot.

She determined to dress me for my wedding, and I was in a tizzy and did not want strangers about me. It was a very simple dress of soft white satin with a chiffon top, a wreathing of orange blossoms and shamrocks (for my husband-to-be was Irish), and his string of pearls.

'You are not superstitious, miss?' asked the lady's maid, 'for they say pearls mean tears.'

What an inspiration she had for saying the wrong thing! 'That's silly!' said I with spirit.

Everyone else went off ahead of me, for suddenly the bride finds herself left alone with her father, and is rather lost and very much alone. So I went down the staircase that I loved, the girl in the white dress which I had dreamt of that first time, but this day the sun did not shine for it was foggy, and I heard the guns at sea.

There was a crowd in the street, for half Walton had turned out to see the fun. Years later, a darling woman said, 'You did not look a day more than fifteen . . .' and I had felt to be all fifty!

I wasn't feeling lovely really, for I had only just recovered from a bad attack of 'flu, and somebody had given me brandy to boost me up. I'm not at my best on brandy, it does extraordinary things to me, and I had started hiccoughs. Appalled, I thought that I could not possibly get married with hiccoughs, though maybe this was exactly what I should have to do.

As the car moved off I turned to look again at Hertford House, and for a moment I thought—ridiculously—that it smiled at me! I always said that I should never take strong drink.

Thalassa
Frinton-on-Sea, Essex

The train was late when we returned from our honeymoon, and Frinton was black as pitch. Arthur fell over the corner of the rockery as we turned into the garden, and when the door opened all the staff was lined up in the hall in an elegant row, with the butler in command, ready to congratulate.

'Not this!' I gasped.

When we had said the right thing, or what we hoped was the right thing, I rushed upstairs to change for dinner. Everybody changed for dinner in the war years. There was a fire crackling in my bedroom promising me all the glorious treats that Thalassa could offer. I must say money is much more congenial to live with than poverty, which pinches and screws all the time. Money pets you up a bit.

I had the inevitable trouble of settling in with all those servants, and Mrs. Bunthorpe struggling for the lead, the lady's maid, and one thing and another. Arthur wished to entertain on the lavish scale, but he did not like paying for it. He had people to dine every night, and expected six courses. They were the mode. There must be game on the menu, too, he refused to be fobbed off with the stout old hen, for he had no place in his heart for stout old hens, it had to be wild duck, or pheasant, or such! His idea of housekeeping money was meagre in the extreme (£6 a week for us all, and I paid the rent from it, too),

for he just had no idea how much food cost. I explained, somewhat haltingly, that game was expensive.

'You must find the way,' said he with dignity, and then, as
the final silencer, 'My ma always did.'

His ma did *not*. She never read a bill because she thought
them common, and she shrank from all financial negotiations as
being vulgar. Her principle was on the first of the month to
issue cheques for this and that, and if the cook got perks from
these she did not care. Never was a woman more diddled.
Poverty had taught me how to housekeep to my own advantage,
and I did find the way out, of course. The cook might be an
aggravating woman, and she was, but she had a father who
made his pocket money by coming across little oddments when
the spirit moved him. The Backwater, which runs between the
Naze and Dovercourt peninsula, and goes far inland, has a merry
colony of wild birds there for the taking. The added attraction
was that the cook's father was far cheaper than the shops.

After this amiable discovery we got along fine.

My young husband should have been indebted to my frugal
upbringing, but not he. 'Never admit it,' was what he said.
Once, when in a more interested mood, 'Didn't you find it
terribly humiliating?'

'Just a darned nuisance,' I told him with truth.

It is a very strange thing that although Thalassa was my great
joy, and perhaps the house I loved best (though privately I still
believe it was for the pride of showing off and very little else),
the house had no personality. The dweller on the threshold and
I never even met. The place made no thumbprint on my self,
and it did not change me. Today I see it as merely a passing of
time, little more. But goodness me, we lived in style, never to
bed before two in the morning, with early parade at seven, so
that it was one big panic.

At Christmas I managed to get my brother home from Egypt
on compassionate leave to see his mother, who was now worse.
He was a corporal and this provided the most sickening com-

plications, for the butler was a sergeant. This, said Arthur, was an impossible situation, and he was right. There was also some ghastly rule of which I had never heard before, under which officers and men could not meet in the same room when in uniform. As everybody *was* in uniform then, this further complication was appalling.

Hurriedly I had to get my brother into civvies, and then half the energetic old ladies of Frinton pushed white feathers on to him, and he said shocking things about them.

That white-feather mania was a very real plague indeed to life.

My mother was still at the small hotel along the front, but weakening. I wanted to get her into Thalassa, where we had empty bedrooms, but Arthur would not have it. He was afraid lest people might tease him about his mother-in-law, and he dug in on this.

I said, 'But if people tease you, why not stand up to them?' which had been part of my own education.

'How can I if it is the C.O.?'

I didn't believe the C.O. would do it. He was an amiable darling (to me) and never fierce, or had I got Conky wrong?

We had a fairly good Christmas and a new year's night when we were all absolutely sure the war would end by Easter. Certainly we were the most optimistic people. We had a big party with charades, everybody dressing up, and the result of that was that one of the captains went home wearing a taffeta petticoat of mine (otherwise in full uniform) and the guard stopped him. This caused some trouble. Conky did not like noisy parties, or an officer who wore his Sam Browne *and* my petticoat and then marched forth down the street believing that he looked lovely!

Early in the new year my brother had to return to Egypt, and that was the most gloomy day. The submarine menace was increasing and we knew that anything could happen, and all the time Mother was getting very much worse. Everything came at once, in the way it does in life; perhaps when you come to think of it, Thalassa was not a lucky house. My husband had a collapse, and for the first time I discovered that he was very ill indeed. His difficult moods, his sudden collapses and black-outs, were not just 'his way', which was how I had glossed over them, but an illness which would (if he lived long enough) destroy him.

That was when I found that I was going to have a baby. I do pick my moments! I thought, as I stood at the window of Thalassa and watched that very grey sea looking unbelievably cold and quite unrelieved.

In March my mother died. When it came, it was allied to so many other tragedies that it seemed that I was suddenly lost in a fog of bewilderment. My husband lost a 'pip'. 'It happens that way to some of us,' he said brightly.

My early training had taught me that it was frightful. My early training called black black and white white, in a way that my new life had never seemed to realise. I said so, and *that* was a mistake.

For a few weeks Arthur was out at Holland Gat in charge of a lone camp, which was sitting there waiting for the Germans to invade us, and then to fight to the last man. This jolly little proposition did not seem to worry them too much, but I should have said that Holland Gat was the most unenterprising spot along the coast. It provided the dreariest walk for me, when I wandered along to visit. I went by the sea wall which bordered the golf links, with the east wind tearing in on me, and a morass under foot. Coming back was no better, for on that walk one always caught the wind whichever way one walked.

I was alone in Thalassa with all the ritual of elaborate meal, butler and maids, and that dismal routine of the butler approaching with 'Sherry, madam?' and Madam saying, 'Water, please.' I never know why it is a crime to drink water, but it is considered to be lowering to the status. The best people don't do it, but I do. Why? I was often asked. The humble excuse 'Because I like it' never cut much ice.

Thalassa was grand, but grand only. It did not change me,

it did not even impress me for very long, for I got the feeling that Thalassa had got me into the biggest muddle of my life, and in that I was not far wrong.

We were moved.

There was one of those dreadful weeks when Arthur went on ahead of me to get a furnished house, in Falmouth of all places; as though they could not find anywhere further away. 'It could have been Lanark,' he said.

He went off to Cornwall and I stayed behind to settle up. My big worry was that Mother had left me her furniture and this was in store, which I disliked for it. I wanted to rent a small house, and get the furniture into the shelter of it, then perhaps later let the house if I had to, or live there when the time came when Arthur went overseas.

Until now, when I wanted a store for the furniture, Frinton had been bursting with empty houses, there were several in every street; now when it came to it there seemed to be none. The limited choice—for time was fast running out—pushed me hard. I found one in Harold Road. Its worst trouble was that its name was Poona, engraved by some clot in the gable, and, as far as I could see, impossible to obliterate.

Poona was a small villa, five beds, three sits, and a tennis court. It stood in a road behind the Esplanade, which I felt was to the good. A winter at Thalassa had told me how very cold the sea front could be.

I took Poona in a hurry. The rent was £75 a year, and the landlord lived one side of me, his son the other, but they were both nice people. Now suddenly Arthur was shot off to Falmouth, and I hardly had the time to get the furniture thrown into the place, certainly no time to sort it out, before I followed him down to Cornwall.

I left Thalassa without a qualm. My loveliest home, my most radiant home, where I had had everything in the world, yet, when it came to it, nothing. As I drove to the station I realised that none of it would ever stay with me now. I had drawn down the curtain.

The same thing was to happen in Falmouth for the next three months. It was just a cottage overlooking the park, a simple little house with a rotten bathroom, which depressed me, and a small garden eternally full of flowers.

Maybe I was born with a cottagey mind, and maybe Thalassa had been the ghost of a dream which was never really me. I was marking time. Just ticking over. What next? I asked.

82 South Croxted Road
Dulwich, SE

This was the unexpected house. It bobbed into my life of a
sudden, for in August we were back in London. Arthur's condition had worsened, and he had to be given a 'soft' job, so he
was transferred to the Ministry of Pensions. This had been
achieved only by string-pulling in a big way. My introduction
to army life had taught me a lot along this line, for one pulled
strings for every single thing one wanted. It would be pleasant
to get back to London, I felt, for Falmouth was just a passing
dream. Again I never met the dweller on the threshold, I cannot
even remember the address. Again it was a house which did
nothing to me (I was getting too many of these), and it left me
as I was when I first entered it.

I thought a lot about Poona. I wondered if Poona might not
be a very different proposition. Not pretty, it was a very ordinary little house of Victorian architecture, and had been built in
1892. Somehow I felt Poona might be helpful.

The moment that Arthur got the job at the Ministry of Pensions we returned to London to Berners Hotel for a week, and
the first thing to do was to find a furnished house where he
could travel to and fro, and where I could have the baby.

On the Sunday we went to have tea with some friends of his
who lived in Dulwich. This was a family of sons, most of whom
had acted as tutors to Arthur and had aided and abetted the
gallant attempt to get him through his matric. He had never been

to school, for my mother-in-law had been alarmed lest he should learn something vulgar, and even Eton was not good enough. I daresay that Eton can be as vulgar as most (for small boys *are* vulgar, and perhaps it does them good), and that was not her idea.

Oh no, said my mother-in-law.

Then, of course, when she wanted him to go to Cambridge and get to the Bar she was up against the horror that he had had no education and Cambridge demanded a certain standard. She rushed round to the Gaylers for help, and this family of sons took him on. I must say that I hand it to them for what they did. Arthur was clever in his own way, he had a good memory, and could absorb learning, but it must have been a big job.

Hugh Gayler had been our best man; I felt that he was the least attractive of the sons, but that, of course, I dared not say. A few months' marriage had taught me to hold my tongue. Privately I was not partial to Hugh, who was a solicitor, and I always felt he had an eye to the main chance. Perhaps most of us have that, but I would give Hugh credit for having it more than most.

Down we went to tea with the family, and there we broke the news of our anxiety to find somewhere suitable to live. I was apprehensive, for I had discovered that I possessed a very extravagant husband. When Arthur had a fiver in his pocket he invariably spent a tenner. He liked it that way, but it was a little tricky to cope with afterwards. It so happened that Hugh knew of a house to let further up South Croxted Road, and he suggested that he and Arthur went to see it.

'What about me?' I asked.

'Oh, you wait here. Mustn't get over-tired,' said everybody blandly.

I was slightly alarmed as to what the two of them might do, but off they went, and they were gone for an unending time. When they returned they smelt of spirits. It had been one of those visits which had become an occasion.

They had taken the house. Just like that, without my even

getting a sight of it, and I was horrified. I suggested that I should now go along to see it. It was getting dark, said they, and the black-out made it difficult. In the end there we were, Arthur and I, driving back to Berners Hotel having taken a new house which I had never even seen, and myself getting annoyed.

I never did see that house until the following week when I drove down with all the luggage to meet the servants there. I admit that it was far better than it looked from the outside, for that is the way with those houses. Three sitting-rooms, five beds upstairs, and an amiable garden at the back. The maids arrived, the dogs, and there we were. After all, I told myself, I have got out of this all right, and it *is* a nice house. But that first night taught me something.

Nobody had said a thing about the R.N.—God bless them— who were fully installed in the Crystal Palace. The air raids were constant, and when the naval guns got going at the Crystal Palace it really was something. Never had I heard such a row! This was no place for a young girl who was going to have a baby, said I, and I am one of those silly women who do not like bangs.

'I hate it,' I said.

My husband said nothing. He never apologised, and I have found that men very much dislike apologies. It gives them the jitters to have to say 'I'm sorry'. This was war, said he, all of us had to share it, and share alike, and what were a few guns anyway?

'If your son arrives with one in his hand I shall blame you,' I said.

Next morning there appeared a very official-looking letter. I recognised the writing. It was from Hugh. My husband opened it, and I must admit that before he pulled himself together he did look surprised. Hugh had sent in a fat bill for 'legal assistance in obtaining the lease of 82 South Croxted Road'. The legal assistance had entailed taking a taxi to it and back.

'That's cheek!' I said.

You know what men are! Loyalty to the old friend becomes a menace with them. 'He has to live,' Arthur observed.

'So have we.'

'He's my dear old friend.'

'A dear old swindle, if you ask me!' I answered.

Those guns got worse. Most of London now spent the nights sitting in their cellars, it became the right formula, but it *was* cold at times, and always uncomfortable.

The best part of 82 was that it introduced me to Barton, who was the most charming chauffeur anybody ever had, and a real joy. Barton had the big Daimler at the garage round the corner, and he attended to our wants. He and I saw life very much alike. Barton used to take us up on our visits to Prince's Gate and wait outside with me whilst Arthur went in. My mother-in-law thought that anyone who was going to have a baby could not enter number 6. My sister-in-law, older than myself, was a spinster. There was also the butler. He had several children of his own, but this did not count, so I must wait outside with Barton.

'Oh well, madam, it takes all sorts to make a world, they say,' said Barton brightly, eyeing the cake and milk sent out to me, with the coldest eye.

'It seems so to me,' I told him.

My relationship with the in-laws was strained and difficult, and there was nothing that I could do about it. The old butler brought me down baby clothes, Arthur's cast-offs, and I gather that when he returned he was made to report on our home. Our home was all right, surely? But unhappily he had discovered that the people next door took P.G.s. (How *do* butlers discover this sort of thing when you do everything in the world to keep it from them?) One of the P.G.s was black, a very nice man, and amiable. I was looking like a haystack, and whilst most people tried to pretend that I wasn't, the amiable black gent said one day, 'You 'ave the very nice so-big baby, yes?' 'Yes!' said I. He had got it in a nutshell.

My mother-in-law was naturally horrified. We must move at once, she said, and blamed me for choosing the house. The choice had had absolutely nothing to do with me, and we had had that row out before, as I explained.

Was 82 the third house which did not influence me at all, and which I never 'knew', or so it seemed? It was not a lucky house, no more than Thalassa or Falmouth had been.

Arthur was rapidly worsening, and finally he had to go to King's College Hospital for treatment. When the baby was born in 82 he was in hospital and too ill ever to return to the Army. They kept that from me for a short time, but that is the sort of news which eventually has to come out, and here it was.

My husband had not got on well with my maternity nurse. Owing to a shocking miscalculation of dates, she was with us a good three weeks before he was born.

'I can't stick that woman,' said Arthur.

Barton commiserated with me. 'That's the way the gentlemen always feel, madam,' said he. 'I've seen it before.'

Barton had been the one who had met Nurse at Victoria and brought her down. Before I ever saw her he had got her and her luggage into the bedroom, and came to report to me. He greeted me with 'We've got somethink here, madam, I should say. It won't be sir's idea at all.'

It was *not* sir's idea!

I tried to keep both sides of the fence, which is always a bad mistake to make. Barton and my husband connived to keep her in the dark about the whisky they were getting into the house, and other little peccadilloes of their own. Really these were no business of hers, but how she argued!

In the end he took her back to Victoria, luggage and all, and came back to report once more to me. 'That's that, madam, we've got rid of her. Now perhaps we can sit back for a bit and take life easy.'

That was not what happened.

My husband had been sent to a convalescent home near Edinburgh; the powers-that-be were geniuses at doing this sort of thing, and nobody could say a word. Their understanding of geography was extraordinary.

Now I had to engage a children's nanny, and the one I got came from the midlands. Barton went off to fetch Nanny from Paddington, and I waited in a panic. I saw her through the curtains and she was the genteel kind; Barton took her upstairs and came down to report yet once more.

'If you ask me, madam, we've got it again!' said he. 'There'll be trouble there! You start as you mean to go on, or she'll be nanny-ing you!'

I began to dislike the house.

Let us come down to harsh facts, I wept more tears in 82 than any house where I had yet lived. The new nanny had charm, she was quite awfully respectable, and so refined, but oh what a woman! ('Here we go!' said Barton.)

She disliked the pram, said it was too shallow, and she must have a larger one. She wanted a bath for the baby. The basin had done for me, but nothing but the best did for Nanny. She disliked the pattern of his vests, and when I asked her to bring him down for his goodnight kiss she said, 'The baby cannot be disturbed, madam.'

At that very moment a yell from his room told me that even if he could not be disturbed he could himself be very disturbing.

'And how are we getting along with the new person, madam?' asked Barton, as he took me off to buy a bath for the baby (you may be sure I had been driven into getting it).

'We aren't,' I said with some bitterness.

'Madam would do well to insist,' he suggested.

'Madam isn't that sort,' I reminded him.

My husband got away from the convalescent home by Christmas, and Barton took me up to King's Cross to welcome him at some unearthly hour in the morning, but put me off taking the baby with me. Maybe he had something there. We drove home believing that all our troubles were at an end (always the sign of worse ahead!), and when we got back

Nanny would not let Arthur see his own son because it was not 'baby's time', whatever that might mean.

Twenty-four hours of Arthur *and* Nanny made me sick to death of the South Croxted Road, and I think the Christmas which we spent there was the most miserable one of my whole life. I even went for a walk in the churchyard of Holy Trinity because I could think of nothing better to do. My husband came and took me away. He felt that I needed some fun, and on the Boxing Day insisted on taking me to dine at the R.A.C. 'to take my mind off things'. Barton had thought it an idea if I went out somewhere. I must say that the visit to the R.A.C. took my mind off things rather more than any of us had expected, for Grandma-in-law came in, and she was a poppet! I always loved old Lady Lurgan, with a small cap on her white hair, and her amused eyes. She was in festive mood, Uncle Billy had dined and wined with her, and now she was gay. Alas, she was deaf and spoke very loudly, and wanted to tell us some stories a charming young man had told her. She didn't know what they meant, of course, but she did know that they were awfully funny and just the stuff for Boxing night! It got a bit much for the R.A.C. and we decided to take her home. Barton helped with this. He was one of those useful people who always on the instant see the plight in which you are, and he did exactly the right thing.

We were very tired as we returned to Dulwich. The new year was round the corner, the year in which the war would end, surely? It now seemed that it had been going on for ever. Arthur was back in civvies, we drank to the future when we got back to 82.

'You know, this house has done nothing for me,' I said.

'How could any house do anything?'

But they had done. The rectory had moulded me, 41 had nearly killed me, Thornlea had cut me to pattern, Hertford House had spoilt me. Now I would turn back to Frinton and I longed for the sound of the sea again, the walks on those firm sands, and the feeling of being in our very own place. I was glad that I had taken Poona, but it is such an awful name, I thought.

All of which goes to show that names don't really matter as we think they do. Barton came for us for the last time. There was some difficulty in getting everyone into the car, the luggage, and this and that. Looking back at 82, it seemed to be such a common little house, but at the last moment, because I was born with a most ridiculous bump of sentimentality, I knew that I did not want to part. Yet I should have hated to stay there another minute.

Years after, I brought my second husband to see it. The next-door house, which was similar in pattern, was being converted into flats, and, as there was nobody about, I nipped round to the back and got in.

'This was the drawing-room,' I said, and with affection as I looked out over the familiar view.

Then when I went out into the hall everything was changed for the transference into flats had made a shocking difference to it all, and I could not find the front door. It seemed to be absurd to be there in a house which I knew quite well and to have lost the front door, and somehow I knew that my husband was laughing at me.

Perhaps, after all, it does not pay to go back in life.

Poona, Harold Road
Frinton-on-Sea, Essex

We got down to Frinton on a bleak January afternoon, and I went across to Poona before the light failed me. I was entering the house where I was to live through the next five, and perhaps the most eventful, years of my life, for in them I myself was to be made. From them I should emerge utterly changed, though I did not know it when I opened the front door with that enormous church key that we had for it, and went inside. It smelt of dampness.

The furniture removers had flung everything down just as they thought they would, and had done as little as they could. It was a ghastly sight, even in the failing light of that moment. Light fog twisted about the leafless trees in the garden. My first reaction was, How shall I ever get this place straight, and when can we hope to move in? Then I thanked God that Arthur had not come across with me and seen it at its absolute worst. I stood in the hall half afraid. Had I made the mistake of my life in taking the place, and was the furniture for ever damaged by it? In that hour it almost seemed to be hopeless.

Three weeks later we had got it straight and aired, which was something, seeing how difficult coal was to get. Everything was approaching the shortest of short commons, but we all worked hard, and I went down to the beach and brought back armfuls of driftwood, to the horror of my husband. He insisted that he would not have a beachcomber for a wife. It had never worried me, and when we lived in Hertford House I brought back wood for the fire every day, loving the blue flames that came from it.

Poona was not a pretty house, it was not even comfortable, but this house changed my life more than any other in which I lived. I knew that it would, the very first night that I slept in it. Mrs. Bunthorpe and Alice Jackson were with us, and, of course, that dragon of the nursery, Nanny. Nanny was the prize nuisance.

I furnished Poona with my mother's things, which Arthur did not like, but his money was running a little short, and it was hopeless to imagine that we could now launch out and buy more furniture. With the war, all prices had gone soaring sky high.

In the end he saw this, and the only detail that he stipulated was that he must have a gas fire for his study, which had a gas-ring attachment to it so that he could fry himself an egg when-ever he wanted it. Until now he had never seemed to be par-ticularly fond of eggs, so that this struck me as being a very peculiar demand. He explained that he had done this in Trintiy Hall and it had delighted him. I found the fried-egg business a positive curse. When he broke them he got them on the carpet, or ruined the sofa (a legacy from Great-Aunt Minnie), and once my dress, for I sat down in the chair where an egg awaiting cooking had got there first. It was a great pity that I ever found a second-hand gas fire fitted with the ring for egg-frying.

Bit by bit we got the house going; it was not a convenient house, it was not even attractive, but it was our first real home.

Arthur's contributions to it shocked me somewhat. He seemed to have gone in for a lot of stuffed birds, which were not my line of country. Then we had unending photographs of groups of flaccid-faced young men at Trinity Hall; tennis, cricket, rugger, boating, all the sporting activities. He had three very large wickerwork chairs which fitted in nowhere, none of which were a great help in smartening up the home.

Spring came early that year, and we got the garden reformed

with much difficulty, for the place had been empty so long that it was in a terrible mess. The tennis court recovered first, and there was a nice little orchard at the far end. We found out later that the interesting-looking trees were nearly all bullaces, which was a bitter disappointment.

By Whitsun I had got rid of Nanny, and her place was taken by Woolly, quite a young girl, who adored children and whom the baby liked tremendously. He thrived. But my husband was getting steadily worse.

The curious thing was that I swung between the wildest hopes that 'something would happen', that absurd desire of the very young, and those moments of complete miasma when I saw ahead all sorts of horrible things. The war was still going badly, sometimes we thought we should never win it, and then what would happen? But we ourselves had got a fixed background behind us in Poona. It might be ordinary, it might be unattractive, but it was definitely ours for some years ahead, and after the here-today-and-gone-tomorrow life of the Army that was something.

In the autumn there came the scourge of influenza. Woolly got it first, but not badly; a week in bed and she was better and up again. Then Mrs. Bunthorpe went down, and she had it very badly, I thought she would die. It was my husband who died with it.

I shall never forget the sudden sense of aloneness as I stood at the top of the stairs on that small square landing with the feeling that nothing would ever be the same again. What do I do? I asked the house. I always had the feeling that somehow the house told me. People thought I'd go right away, but where could I go? and I was sick of wandering about. We all need the stout firm background of walls which stand around us and are *there*. An end of one phase is always the beginning of another. Ahead lay what?

Just for a few months I did not really find myself. I went to the Officers' Home with other V.A.D.s, but knew that this was nothing more than a passing thing. Something would happen

F

and show me the way, I believed, and the way had not come yet. With midsummer my brother returned from Egypt. I had always wondered what we should say to each other when we met after all this time, when so much had happened; then when we did meet, he having come by an earlier train and walking down Connaught Avenue right into me, the first thing he said was 'I've lost my tommy's cooker.'

I cried!

Joscelyn did not think much of Poona, maybe he was right, but already it was somewhere I had lived for over a year, somewhere where I felt I had roots. Small ones, it is true, but roots. I wasn't settling down. I had the feeling that I had missed something, I had lost time perhaps, experiences perhaps, something which I needed, and had to find before I could go on. It is rather difficult to explain how this comes to one, but it does come.

Then, in the late summer, I found it.

The craze for dancing had burst on the world. It was new, it was gay after a long period of strain, monotony and war weariness. Perhaps the idiotic belief that we had done with war for ever inspired it, but quite suddenly we wanted desperately to dance. It was the era of *Swannee, How I love you! How I love you! Missouri*, and *Widows are wonderful*, which too many people applied to me.

Perhaps the fact that my brother's return brought with it a sense of security, and I was no longer alone, started me off. There was an absurd summer night when we went to Victor's, danced and came home at one in the morning down Connaught Avenue still dancing. A night when we went down to the huts and cooked bacon and eggs and made hot coffee, and still danced there to a gramophone on the 'high wall'. With that music, and that movement, and something which seemed to be the very inspiration of youth itself, all those hard years when I should have been dancing, became matterless and nothing. The cinema, nursing Mother, poverty, hardship, and intense flagellating anxiety, all went.

With the dawn, and not even tired, I danced into Poona and in the soft pink of a hazy morning it looked almost romantic. I went back to seventeen, *right back*, and I began all over again.

I had never shut the rectory gate on girlhood at all. That part which came after I left was a nasty dream which had gone, and I had awakened. Perhaps for the first time I was worry-free, and could be happy again.

Those were the two perfect summers.

Frinton had come into its own, exciting actors and actresses were there, Leslie Henson, Nelson Keys, Ivor Novello, Gladys Cooper.

> It'll be all the same, just the same,
> A hundred years from now;
> No use a-worrying, no use a-flurrying,
> No use kicking up a row. . . .

Chitter-chatter, scandals, thrills and excitements. 'Do you know that Gladys Cooper is sitting in her garden and Ivor Novello is combing out her hair? She looks wonderful.' 'Seymour Hicks has just gone up Connaught Avenue on a tricycle for a bet.' 'Nelson Keys has taken the hut next to my own,' from me, 'and he dropped the baby the other morning.'

I had the money for frocks, I had established myself, and now could enjoy just every hour. Of course, there were men who wanted to marry me, who probably did not realise that my husband had left me his money on the condition that I did not re-marry, and anyway why should I want to? A girl is happier free, said I.

Motor-bikes were everywhere. If one was anyone, one had to get into Colchester in eighteen minutes from our level crossing, otherwise one was out of date. We danced all the time, I believed that we should go on dancing for ever.

But if you come back to live your teens when you are older, the impetus does not last so long. One night I woke up to that.

It was at a dance at Victor's club, and in the last foxtrot I got tired. It wore thin. The man was a bore, and last night he had been exciting, but tonight he had lost his charm. I walked home alone, which was something new for me, and as I walked I thought, for no reason that I could fathom at the time, I'll have to grow up.

The careless years were over. I had lived through them, and out of the happiness and the freedom and the wild sense of living *for the first time*, I grew up properly.

I can do something more than this, I said.

I would go back to reality, and reality lay in my writing. I realised that now was the real start, it had to be now or never. I had tried before and had failed, but this time I would put into it all that I had got, and would try so hard that I simply couldn't fail, or so I thought.

'Waste your youth on a silly thing like writing?' said Frinton. 'You'll never do it. You have to be clever to write.'

So that was what they thought of me!

That was when I began another version of my own story, at Poona, and this time it began with 'Once upon a time . . .'

I got some introductions out of thin air, I bought myself a season ticket to London, and I started to attack Fleet Street my own way. At least, I told myself, aware that I was exciting more than a little comment, I may not be clever, but I have got guts, and guts are the things that count.

I began at the bottom of the ladder, for I have always believed that this was the lasting way to work up. I wrote for all the wrong papers, for at that time it had to be anything rather than nothing. I worked hard, because I had got to make up for lost time, and I knew that I could not afford to delay. Frinton thought that I had gone mad. They had condemned the eternal dancing, and the gay happiness which had come to me, now they condemned my idea of launching myself into the literary world. But they comforted themselves with the sublime idea that it was bound to be temporary only, and, of course, it could never succeed.

At Whitchurch I had been so sure of being a writer. The Shottery Road had set me back and had dimmed my foresight. At Thornlea the cinema had for the time being squashed it. Hertford House had been encouraging, but during my married life I had done nothing at all. It seemed absurd that Poona—that rather ordinary little place—after all, had done it.

In the summer after I started, one day there came the first sign of progress. Fleet Street is not keen on interlopers. I found the going hard, I had to fight for every line, though I had good friends there, those men who in the very early days made me go on; Frank Lamburn, Leonard Crocombe, Hessel Tiltman, Freddy Lidstone, men who kept me hard at the grindstone. They did much for me. But one summer day in the garden of Poona I suddenly knew that I was really going to make good. I was sitting with my small son in the arbour.

When Thalassa was sold up I went to the sale with the idea of buying some small souvenir. Never did goods go for such high prices. An ordinary little picture, which I should have thought a guinea would cover, fetched over £500, and staggered me. The red turkey carpet in the dining-room brought in £200. It ended with the fact that the only thing that I could buy was the arbour out of the garden which went for ten bob.

It was not too easy to get a large square arbour home to Poona, but in the end I got four men to say they would do it on their way to work one day. Two mornings later I woke to the sound of most appalling language rising from the side path below my bedroom window. Poona had very narrow paths on either side of it and ill-advisedly these men were trying to bring the big arbour into the garden this way. Trees crashed, and branches broke, but in the end they staggered through on to the lawn, and got it set up on the edge of the bullace orchard. I used to have tea there in summer, for those were the years when tea was a necessity, in fact life would have been quite incomplete without it.

On this particular afternoon the baby and I were having our tea there when Woolly came out of the house with a telegram in her hand. It had been dispatched to me by a London editor and was nothing more or less than the royal command.

> Please come here tomorrow at three. I have a matter to discuss with you.

My reply was 'Yes, please.' I sat for the rest of that day in a daze with the editorial telegram in my lap, and Poona at the far end of the lawn with its silly name engraved in the gable and the trees stirring on either side. This could, I knew, be the beginning of everything. That was exactly what it was!

I spent five years altogether in Poona. Almost everything happened there, but the house which was inauspicious to look at, impersonal, one would have thought, and almost a little vague, did everything for me. First of all when the servant problem became so much more tricky, we had to do away with the cook and manage with one general maid, and a nanny. This meant that I was introduced to weekly cooking days. I turned to and made cakes for the week, puddings and galantines, and so have a store in the large cool larder on which to draw.

My mother had been a very good cook who could accomplish the most startlingly exciting dishes when she wished, but I had not turned to it before. Poor Arthur would have had a fit at the idea of any woman who bore his name doing anything quite so vulgar. But times change, and although I did not know it then, they were changing a little faster than I appreciated.

I settled myself in to the one afternoon at the kitchen table; it was the old-fashioned square table, with a dresser and all the blue plates in the world, with copper pans, and with the glimpse of the garden beyond. The baby was always installed in a corner; there was nothing he liked better than cooking days, for he was then the dish-licker-in-chief. Iced cakes were what he demanded. Iced cakes brought him infinite joy. One always had to do at least one of them, if only to interest the baby.

My launching out in this direction was quite a mistake. I was good at it. My brother's hungry friends flocked in to tea when my Dundee cake was there, and the soda cake which I adored, and particularly the home-made bread. I have invariably found that bread is the one thing that men prefer to anything else, and there is great joy in baking it. I made a lot of what is known as soda bread. In the rectory we had once had a old Irish cook, passed on to us by the parson at Ilmington, and if you ask me I should think he was glad to be rid of old Fanny. But she would work like a black, and she made the bread.

This was the Irish soda bread which is so delicious, and for ever afterwards in our house there was always a loaf of it hanging about somewhere, long after we had got rid of Fanny, for we handed her back to Ilmington with our love and a blessing, and the bread was the treasure that she left behind her.

Somehow that afternoon working in the kitchen brought me a new angle on life. Poona had put the love of home into me. I developed a pride in certain cakes I made, certain puddings, and a steak-and-kidney pudding which had orange in it, and which was quite divine, every man's joy.

But Poona was not for ever.

The landlord died one Christmas; it never struck me at the time that his demise could make a difference to me, but it did. I still had my lease to run out, and I knew, of course, that there was a tremendous difficulty in getting houses, for since the war there had been this problem. Although building was going on everywhere (for there is nothing like a war to produce shocking building, and we had those pale mushroom-pink bricks and asbestos tiles popping up), naturally the demand was setting the prices rising.

I was offered Poona for £1100. It might just as well have been the earth to me. So someone else bought it, and the new landlady immediately sent me a notice to quit. Because I didn't do this, thinking I was safe, she served a writ on me. It was something of a jar to see the amiable policeman, hot and perspiring, standing on the verandah mat.

'I'm very sorry about this, madam,' said he.

'What have I done?' I asked.

'You haven't done nothing, madam. It's a shame,' and off he went.

I rushed off to Nick about it. He was not alarmed, and the affair was fought out at Manningtree, where a most extravagant counsel defended me. I went there in cold horror, and I *was* alarmed when I heard what he had to say about me.

'This poor child,' said he, indicating my person (and I had thought myself so grand!) 'She lost her husband in the war, has a brother back from fighting in the East, and a baby under two years old. She needs a home for them. The new owner needs that home only as a summer holiday abode.'

I won my case. I saw myself in a new vein and came out of the witness-box in great surprise. But, of course, the moment my lease ran out the landlady would come down on me and get herself into Poona. It was time that I looked about me.

It was Nick's idea that I should build myself a little bunga-low of my own, and I realised that this might be a big help. I had always wanted to own my house, not understanding the complications it could produce. I applied to my trustees to see if they could help, but my trustees were haughty. They washed their hands of the whole thing. They were the sort of superb aristocratic trustees (the men wore astrakhan collars to their pompous overcoats), and disliked talking about money, feeling that it was degrading. Nick introduced me to a building society, and I must say that that was a very different story.

I found two plots of land for sale within my means, always the big problem, and as far as I can see this is everybody's problem though they never care to discuss it. One was in the Old Road, which I had never liked, and it had a garrulous friend living there who was hard enough to escape without living next door to her. No, said I. The other was in Pole Barn Lane, which is the common end of Frinton (if Frinton ever admits to having a common end). For me it was near to the station, and on a cold winter's night walking back after a heavy day in town was galling. I went on to this wild patch of land which one day would be my garden; I picked two marguerites and some gorse, and brought them home as special treasures. I can't think why, but I am that sort of fool.

I bought the plot.

I thought it would be thrilling when the builders got at it, but I must say they made it look worse than I had ever imagined possible. The thrill died out of the adventure. Every time I went to see how it was getting on, it was *not* getting on. The outlines of the rooms-to-be looked pimping and small. The garden was in an intolerable mess, and plainly the builders did not want me there. Each time when I returned to Poona I wished that I could stay there for ever. Surely I could have raised the £1100? I could have sold the piano. I had some bits of jewellery. Maybe a spare grandfather clock? But unhappily these trivial details do not go as far as one would hope towards £1100. Money *is* money.

In the end I saw a squat little bungle which smelt of cement, and 'bungle' was the right word for it! All around it was a miserable expanse of raw earth. The men had trampled it right down, and I felt we should never escape from the hallmarks of their work. It was hideously untidy, and I had walked across the wet cement of the verandah to investigate, and *that* was a mistake; it was to bear my footprints for ever.

Apparently I had paid only for the bare bungle. All these things like fence and gate were extras. Now what? Bang goes the piano! said I. There was a wild rallying round to get money out of surplus wedding gifts wrapped in black tissue paper in the silver cupboard, because since we lost the butler they had taken so much time to clean. On the back of my brother's motor bike (the sidecar laden with trophies which we had for disposal) I went to and fro to sell them in Clacton. There was no pop-shop in Frinton, and I didn't want Walton to know. There is to this day a certain sense of indignity about the hour when you offer a trinket across the counter to an unsympathetic old man with 'I wonder if you could give me something on this?'

It's annoying, because there is nothing wrong in popping the goods. It is the honest means of raising money, but it is so common, as someone said. She had found out what I was doing, and made the most of it.

The bungalow was already a worry. It could be a greater one, I thought, though the inspiration of popping this and that would be something. I was getting cold feet. And the curious thing was that I was far sorrier to part with Poona than I should have believed possible. It was such an *encouraging* house. I had never really liked it, it had no airs and graces, and we had got black-beetles in the larder, but somehow or other Poona had got into my bones. Here I had found youth again; I had started my literary career; I had discovered cooking and the real love of home, of lavender in the linen cupboard, and clean papers on all the shelves. The insidious joy of washing paint clean and glittering, and of making the place smell clean. When I said *adieu* to it, I wept.

It was a cold day when I walked out with the white cockatoo tucked inside my coat because he had refused to go with any-body else. 'No,' said Cocky. We walked up Harold Grove. I was alarmed as to what he would do, but after a bit he settled down, and then found it good fun to bark merrily at every dog we met. It was the most ghastly experience to have a barking cockatoo nestling to the bust inside the coat, for infuriated dogs leapt on me, and then Cocky yelled out all his best rude remarks.

'Germans! Germans!' shrieked he, which was always his final attack.

I walked through the squelching mud into the new bungalow. The walls were sweating badly, the fire did not seem to be really hot. I shall never like the place, I thought sadly, but was thankful to put Cocky down.

'Bad house,' was his first remark. Hardly encouraging, I must say.

In the end we got his stand unpacked and stuck him on it. We got all the fires going, and they only seemed to make the walls sweat more, and this at the beginning of the winter, too. Poor old Poona, I thought, all alone tonight with nobody there, and I felt quite mad. Of course, the bungalow would be more convenient, and give far less work, but I had never lived in a brand-new house before. My homes had always had associations with the past, this had nothing. The thought worried me. Could it be perhaps that I should find that I had left behind at Poona something that I could not afford to lose? Do houses matter that much?

'Damn! Damn! Damn!' said Cocky from his stand, and scattered a few more peanut shells on to the floor. I was feeling rather that way myself.

Storyette, Pole Barn Lane
Frinton-on-Sea, Essex

I really had no choice about moving, I had had to get out, to allow my landlady to get in, and as I had built this place it was no good having second thoughts now. I called it Storyette, for my stories had built most of it. 'Why not "Novelty"?' asked facetious friends, but as yet the first novel was to come. I brought half of it with me from Poona, and once we had got over the shock of the move, then I would get down to it.

I had not realised that the design of Storyette was one of hundreds, for this was the prevalent pattern in the neighbourhood. A house which is one of hundreds that are similar loses personality, and I ought to have known this.

Just at first it enclosed me with debt in a quite terrifying way, for nobody had explained that the original price did not cover a lot of things which I should have thought were vitally necessary to life therein. Here was Storyette stuck on a mud-trodden waste of wild land, with no fence round it (and the council insisted on a fence), no gate to it, no handles on the doors, and when we came to look into it many other details which I had never thought could be overlooked.

The day I moved in I had said to myself, Well, that ends the expense, thank God, but it did nothing of the sort. There was plenty more to pay.

I got the cheapest fence put up, and bought a second-hand gate, which at least enclosed us. But how depressing is a bleak stretch of wild land where the builders have left a ghastly impression, and there still remain wallops of cement mixing, brick-ends and such! A landscape gardener called and asked if he could help. But he wanted three figures for it, and I had not got three figures left. The curious thing is that although in most lives at some time or other this problem confronts them, they never believe you when you say it is happening to you. He went off in a huff.

In the end my brother and I did the garden, working day and night at it. We designed a garden to delight my little son. It was the garden for a child, which nobody else had ever made, because I like things that way. If there were dozens of beastly looking little bunaglows like mine dotted about Essex there was only one such garden, and we broke our backs working on it.

I started with the small oak tree at the gate, fixing a little platform in it with steps leading up to it. It was a look-out, and bore the name H.M.S. *Ingenious*. We got some gravel down on to those shocking paths, and came round to the front which was at the back of the house, so to speak, so that the sitting-room windows looked up the garden, and in November, just after the move-in, a pretty terrible sight that garden was!

I got a piece of lawn down, suitable for a wigwam encampment, and managed to fix a crazy path right up towards the toolshed at the far end. Now at last we had somewhere where we could walk. I bought a cheap line in trellis work, for I wanted to break the garden into three separate lots (good for hide-and-seek). In the second little garden was a round pond too shallow to drown oneself in, but excellent for paddling and for sailing boats. I laid a wide brick path to surround this, which would take clockwork trains, then flower-beds of tallish flowers to conceal the young from watchful eyes. The arbour which I had bought at the sale of Thalassa came along with us; we made an enormous mound to stand it on, with steps approaching it. The bricklayers had left us a mound which we did not know what to do with, and suddenly we got this idea. The arbour became a castle on the top of a hill. It flew its own flag, and was fitted with a portcullis. I remembered the joys of the portcullis at Warwick Castle when I was a child, and I wanted to bring that thrill here for my own son. On the third section we put more grass and the dead ordinary swing and seesaw. But I had one remarkable difference; I bought a large cracked sewer pipe, and sank this into the far lawn, with entrance and exit clear. It was an escape; a child could fly down it and no adult could follow.

It was a wild success.

Looking back I feel that the bungalow did little for me, it was just a home by the way, a roof and four walls and little more. But the piece of land which I planned became part of me, and still today holds something of myself.

How the walls sweated! We had moved in far too soon, of course, but Christmas got in the way and hurried us. One starts these things in a gay moment, then has to go on. It was more comfortable than Poona in that here the bath *did* work well, for it had a geyser, and one could have ten hot baths running if one so desired (Poona's always ran cold). The kitchen on the other hand was too small; baking afternoons were limited, jam-making evenings a bit of a mess. 'And where do I sit to lick out the bowls?' asked Pip, for this mattered to him.

Storyette ran easily, but it had none of the background that other houses had had. I actually fretted for Poona. It was even more annoying that the new owner had managed to get the name out of that gable, and today it had become Iona.

To Storyette my first novel contract arrived, and that was a moment! Hutchinson had held the Mss. for weeks, and I had assumed that they had lost it, for I always think the worst. Then one icily cold morning, out of the blue flashed this contract! I stared bewildered. I could not believe my eyes. This was IT! I no longer felt the nor'-easter blowing in and I pranced out into the garden, my heavenly contract in my hand. I gavotted round in a whirl of ecstasy. It was a mercy that there were only allotments on either side of me, not houses with watchers over short blinds, for they would have thought me mad. I had a contract at last! And, oh joy, a book of mine was about to be born!

Storyette had convenience and was close to the station, but let us admit the truth, it was shoddy. It was the post-war product of cheap woodwork, cupboard doors which had to be coaxed, and every window got stuck at some time or other. The place seemed to delight in teasing me by keeping all manner of nasty little jokes of that kind up its sleeve for me.

The big lounge was a pleasant room, but I had not realised that it was really the gangway which went through the bunga-low. I wrote there, and interruption is irritating. It was hard at vital moments to have a distressed maid peering round the door and saying in an agitated voice, 'I don't want to upset you, madam, but the sausages haven't come yet,' and because it was a gangway I couldn't bar her entrance.

My brother and I discussed this.

I had played tricks with the original design, asking for the verandah beyond the windows to be larger and wider than the plan. This had been done. 'That's got to be another room,' said I.

It was, I confess, a bit of a bodge, but he and I built a low wall round the verandah, leaving space for a door. My brother was one of those men who are geniuses with their hands, and I was bricklayer's mate. We bought second-hand windows (for there was an amiable builder down the road), and perched these on the new wall. The builder was interested, and he did the roof for us, which was the trying part, for it must be watertight; I had never known the difficulties of making a roof watertight. The new room looked charming, and would fill the bill. We had done the right thing.

'It's a good thing you got rated before you did this one!' said the builder with a smirk. I had been innocent of that danger.

My real trouble was that I had built a place I could not afford, and going short on details is not really wise. Nick told me that later, as I paid off the building society, it would become easier. I only hoped that he was right.

For the moment I saw no chance of paying off the building society, and the debt looked like hanging round my neck for ever.

I had wanted lattice windows, but not being able to afford them at the time, now realised that I could not have them. I had put up a shed to take the motor-bike, in the part of the garden which was on to the road. Then I found that I had trespassed over the building line (which I had never even heard of) and should have asked permission. It was a silly mistake, but we did not have building lines at Whitchurch, and how was I to know they even existed? I found out in the extravagant manner.

The added expense of taking down the shed we had just put up, and transferring it somewhere else, put paid to lattice windows. One day, I told myself, but that day never came.

Yet again I had made that dreadful mistake which seemed part of my life, of coming to live in a neighbourhood where I was out of touch. Pole Barn Lane let rooms in summer (which, of course, was not really done in Frinton), it was slightly artisan in outlook. I should have loved to let rooms if only for the income they would have provided, but I did realise that my friends would never stand for it. Being poor was a disgrace, and Frinton was no place for people who were badly off. I had already discovered that the unforgivable sin there was not to be rich.

'I hope I'll get used to it,' I told Nick.

He hoped so, too, for at that time houses were becoming much more difficult to get, which, as he said, meant that though the bungalow would sell well, if I wished to part with it, it would be hard to get another somewhere else.

'But your train journey to London and back is too much for you,' said he; 'you spend hours in the train; what about going nearer to London?'

I had not thought of that. Somehow on that night when Mother and I first walked down Walton front, with the cliff unguarded on the right, I had become deeply fond of this part of Essex. I adored Walton. I had never thought of leaving the

neighbourhood, for I had been there a long time now, but, as
Nick mentioned it, the idea of going nearer to my work became
a proposition.

'You're going on writing?' he asked.

'Yes, of course. I love it.'

'Some people have funny tastes!'

'It was born in me,' I explained, and that is one of the hardest
things to make people understand. One can be dedicated. There
can be a love within one which fights on whatever happens, and
criticism and others' opinions cannot uproot it, for it is entirely
oneself. But Storyette was not the best place in which to write,
and I had found that out on the very first day I had sat down at
Great-Aunt Minnie's bureau with my typewriter before me.
What did I do?

Maybe it was that the modern bungalow had no ancestry, no
past history, no reflection which others had left behind them,
and nothing on to which I could hold. Mother always said that
in houses previous tenants leave their loves or their hates behind
them. If you were the right sort of fey mentality, then you could
tune in to their emotions; they helped you, or they failed you.
Here in Storyette there was nothing. Oh, ill-named bungalow,
you had *no* story!

I had worked myself to death getting the garden for my child
planned and ready; that done, we had then gone for the verandah
room, not to mention the building, taking down and re-putting
up of the motor-bicycle shed. I felt enraged that on my own piece
of land I was not allowed to put it where I wanted it, but there
it was. For all this energy, and love, and wishful thinking, poor
little Storyette had nothing to give back.

By summer the garden was lovely, for I had treated it to a
simple ruse my father had always used when hard-up. He made
what he called a Friendship Garden; his friends contributed the
plants, and very useful they were. One friend in Second Avenue
offered a fir tree, saying that I could have it if I could get it to
the bungalow. She thought that a great joke! I went round to
nice Mr. Smith's vegetable shop, and borrowed his handcart for

G

the evening, after which it was too simple. Naturally Frinton was horrified, for the greatest fault of the place was that it had not been hard-up. It had never realised, either, that ignorance is one of those boulders which block the road to progress more than any other.

'Are you going to stay on here?' Nick asked me when late summer came. I was making pumpkin jam at the time, and he was waiting for a jar to cool, so that he could take it home with him. They were about to build a memorial hall or something of the kind on the allotment next to me. Perhaps I had chosen the wrong plot, it would be like me to do that.

'No, I don't think I can. I know the place was too cheap, but I couldn't afford more.'

He stood there looking at me, the whole house smelling of pumpkin jam. 'If only those rotten trustees of yours had helped, and they could have done! Five hundred pounds would have meant that the place worked. As it is, it's a bodge.'

'And what do I do with a bodge now?'

The pumpkin jam had cooled, and I was wrapping up a pot for him. He watched me. 'You're far more domesticated than the outside world knows,' he said, 'almost like two different girls in one.'

'All the same, *what* do we do with the bodge now?'

'I'll think that over.'

Next severe winter when every pipe in Frinton froze, and I believe that Poona was chaotic, we had no tragedy, for our pipes had been laid underground. Nick did this for me. He had steered me through dire circumstances and I owe him a great deal. I know he disapproved of the writing, and would have preferred me to marry a visiting millionaire, or a duke (we had the occasional duke), but I was not thinking of re-marriage. I had been deeply hurt when Arthur died.

The golf club had held a sweep on the length of time that I should stay a widow. The man who had got the ticket which said six months thought he was on something good. Stupidly someone told me of this, and I wept bitter tears. Now time was creeping on, and I was not re-marrying. All the affairs had been trivial, the passing amusement, no more. Nobody really realised this.

With early spring I had a bad cold which laid me very low. Maybe I had tried to mix dancing all night with writing all day, and the two did not fit in very well. I went down to Plymouth for a long week-end there. I knew a young officer in the *Royal Oak*, and she was coming in from her spring cruise; so, leaving Joscelyn in charge at home, I went down there. Spring had come to Plymouth, there were flowers everywhere. And that was how I met Robbie.

He was a paymaster lieutenant; he walked into my friend's cabin one day when we were eating stale éclairs (he had a trick of keeping them in the waste-paper basket, which was not a working proposition). 'Do you like stale éclairs?' Robbie asked.

I was rather surprised that he knew.

The young officer dined with me at the Royal that night, leaving early (it could not have been too soon), and we walked out of the dining-room to see Robbie and a brother officer having drinks in the lounge. One of Robbie's biggest faults is that he cannot hide his feelings. He saw my bored face and burst into a roar of schoolboy laughter. *He* had wished to dine with me, my friend had bragged about being asked, very depressing for Robbie, but now he knew that the evening had been a failure.

If you have ever heard Robbie laugh (properly) you'll know exactly what it did to me. I pranced across to him. 'You know that he's a bore?' said I.

'And how!' said Robbie. Ha! ha! ha! again.

What a darling man! thought I. Robbie's number was up on a single laugh.

We wrote to each other, and he wanted to come down to Frinton, but I did not want him at Storyette. I felt that he would hate it, and there I was right. Robbie had very little conception of depths, surfaces mattered to him, and already I knew that Storeyette was not my surface.

The bungalow was now going wrong. There was chimney trouble first, following an enormous log fire we had had at a Christmas party, which made the party look convivial but cracked the hearth for us. This house does *not* like me, I thought.

Then there was drain trouble, and kitchen-sink trouble, all the domestic bothers one after another. It is not much good having the best Mme Herriots in Frinton blooming in your garden when the drains are wrong!

I was suddenly doing much more work in London, with the commissions clogging up my desk; Great-Aunt Minnie's bureau was in a mess. It was difficult to cope with all this, and then return at night to the washing, the brass-cleaning, or something of that sort. I got my household to bed by ten-thirty, if I had any luck at all, and then sat down to type out what I had written in the train. I am prompt. I pride myself that I am the author on whom a newspaper can rely, for I will never let it down. Frank Lamburn (*Pearson's Weekly*) once taught me, 'You may never be a first-class writer, but you can always be reliable, and long after I have gone some editor will bless you for it.'

Originally I was Lamburn-trained, and I have always tried to bear his advice in mind. He was a charmingly kind man, and he did put my feet on the first rung of the ladder, bless him!

I worked better late at night in Storyette because then the place did not intrude so much. It had not been as encouraging as Poona was. When things went wrong Poona could be comforting, it possessed a certain sweet solace of its own. When anything went wrong in Storyette it was the bully who said, 'Yah boo! What did I tell you?'

In the dim background of my life stood Robbie, laughing and saying 'Lovely!' to almost everything, and he influenced me, though I don't suppose he had a clue that he was doing this. His people lived at Otford in Kent, his father had restored the Old Parsonage (I was alarmed as to what he would think of Storyette), and it was one of those show-places that glossy magazines write about. Robbie's innocent talk of it horrified me.

'If you sold the bungalow now, you'd get a good price for it,' said Nick. It had cost £650. In later years it sold for over £2000! Lord! What fools these mortals be!

I offered it for sale.

One day, an unfortunate day when the lounge chimney had caught fire, as it did if it could, and we were blinded with gusts of smoke from it, a rather limp-looking couple arrived and asked if they could see over it. What moments people choose! I thought. 'Tomorrow?' I suggested somewhat dimly, never thinking that they would return. The smoke had done a lot of harm, and Doris the maid (and she was a pet) and I had to clean out the whole room before tomorrow came. Even then it still smelt of smoke. It almost seemed as if Storyette was determined to be aggravating.

I did not think that the limp-looking couple would return, but they did. I ushered them in, and in the most ghastly deadly silence we went round the house together. I made all the usual remarks. 'This is the bathroom. The pipes are underground, so you will never freeze up, which is a help in this part of the world.' No reply. 'This is the kitchen, I have the linen cupboard here, it is so cosy,' which was a lie, for it had been a curse, and half the sheets smelt of boiled cabbage. Again not a word. They hate it! I thought. I showed them Doris's bedroom. 'Compact,' said I, which was a diddle if ever there was one. Pip's nursery-bedroom, and then we came back to the verandah. I only wished they'd go. Nobody said a word, and I was getting sick of them, so I hurried it.

'Just think it over and let me know,' I said, and opened the door with a flourish.

'We want it,' said the woman. That was her first remark, and I could have swooned.

'But you can't want it!' I said, which was scarcely tactful. I had come to the conclusion that they were dumb, or dotty, or just doing it for fun, or something which I did not understand.

There was no trying to beat me down over the price (I had added an extra £50 for luck, and this time I had the luck, thank God!) They did not argue. Later I found that mine was the only bungalow at that low price in Frinton, for—let us admit the truth—Frinton did not go in for cheap bungalows, and this was what they wished to spend. Maybe they had some invalid, or someone who could not take stairs, and one floor only was essential to them; it could have been anything, but they paid what I asked, and never said another word. Not that they had said too much originally. This is too easy, said I. Could they have possession in six weeks? Easily, I said. Yes, of course.

The truth was that my cheap little bungalow standing on a bit of wild land had been no good to me. I was selling it at exactly the right moment. It was 1925.

I had not appreciated that shortage of houses had made them hurry, but the same shortage pushed me into a very nasty corner. I wanted somewhere about thirty miles from London, so we left Doris in charge of Pip, and Joscelyn and I took the motor-bike and did a tour round to find somewhere to live. I did not wish to purchase.

'We are bound to find somewhere,' I said with optimism.

We clucked our way round London, the Buckinghamshire hills, the Thames Valley, Ascot, the Garden of England, etc., living on pots of tea and ham sandwiches in cafés. We came back to Essex more than worried, for everyone had told us that Essex was the most likely place, because it was a county nobody liked. When I said that I did they assumed the expression of those who privately think you are mad but are too polite to put it into words.

We arrived in Harlow, then countrified, with none of this new town, and it had a large park to which I eventually had access. The agent was kind, and said he had not got a single house to let, but he had half a house, which he thought I'd like. 'It's old, you know,' he said, 'and you look the right kind for old houses.'

I think he had got something there.

The Old House stands in the square at Harlow today, and is of Jacobean origin. The garage was in my half. The drawing-room was charming, the dining-room dark, and a nice little study would do for my work. This opened on to the back hall with a staircase winding upwards from it. The price asked was low. Upstairs there were eight bedrooms and a bath which worked, always my first enquiry these days. Eighty pounds a year was the rent, rates trifling. It had been admirably separated, and offered no difficulties of any kind, in fact it was the house I wanted.

Coming from somewhere brand new, obviously I liked somewhere old, as the agent had foreseen. I stood alone in the small study whilst my brother went round the house again with the agent, and I looked across the back hall to the winding staircase and wondered what I ought to do. Was half a house better than none? I was assured that the landlord who lived next door was nice. As I debated, not wanting to rush my hurdles which I had done too often to date, the most extraordinary thing happened. I have told this before, but it has to be repeated for it was part of that house. I saw myself coming down the stairs carrying a very young baby in my arms. I was wearing a frock which at the moment was at home at Storyette, and it happened in a flash, almost as if I had turned on a film of the future.

What on earth did it mean?

Was this a premonition? Was I to marry and have a baby here? Preferably not, for when my son was born in Dulwich I had so nearly died that the thought was not inspiring. The surgeon had warned me, 'Never do this again, for next time you *will* die!'

I had no wish to do this.

Yet here I was coming down the stairs with a baby in my arms, a living baby too, for I had seen it move. Then it had gone! I did not know what to do. I told my brother in the empty drawing-room, a truly lovely room but impossible to heat, as I discovered later. He thought I had had a dizzy fit! Or was I tiddly? Or just thinking out a new story perhaps? Anyway he dismissed the whole thing for what it was worth. Bosh!

Needs must when the devil drives, and I had sold Storyette in a hurry, believing that it would be the only chance to do so. I had to house my brother who had been good to me, one small son, and also Doris whose husband was a gardener at Frinton golf club. I went over the house again without a single uncanny impression. I must have dreamt it. So I signed the lease. I returned to Frinton and hurriedly packed the things for a move. I should deeply regret leaving the sea, of course, for the sea has always been my friend (save when travelling on it in unsteady boats, when it is *not* my friend at all), but I did rejoice to be rid of Storyette, though in these few months I had published my first novel there (with a tea party to celebrate) and now had a contract for other novels. I had gone up in my own little world, though very much down in houses. I had started in Frinton with Thalassa the splendid, and I left it with Storyette, the miserable little squit of a bungle that had been a bodge.

On the last night of all I slipped down Harold Road and said goodbye to Poona over the hedge. A new owner was there now, and I doubted if she would be of a sentimental nature which would understand my tender farewell to it.

I went down to the sea at midnight, it was low tide with that heavenly scent of ozone everywhere, and I said goodbye to that. In a hut a gramophone played and I wanted to dance. 'One day I'll come back here, I hope,' I said, then suddenly, with bold assurance, 'Yes, of course I'll come back.'

Dower House
Harlow, Essex

I re-named my half of the house the Dower House, which seemed fitting seeing that I was a widow. I arrived there about midday on a June morning, driving the Lagonda myself to the peril of all, for I am the world's worst driver. I had Doris and Pip with me, two cats and a dog, whilst my brother led the pilgrimage on the motor-bike with the goldfish in the sidecar and the cockatoo saying shocking things as they travelled. Cocky hated moves. 'Bad house! Bad house!' he screeched.

We drove through the summer lanes, lacy with cow-parsley and sweet with the first rosebuds. It was to be the easiest move of my life, for going from a bungle to a capacious house is so simple. By four that afternoon tea was served to me in the drawing-room with the flowers done and everything over. The furniture looked quite beautiful. Those portraits of my ancestors who had sneered down from the bungalow walls now conformed to pattern. Perhaps all authors are sensitive to atmosphere, but I knew that the Dower House had some of the graciousness of Hertford House, and being summer I did not guess that its trouble was that nothing on earth could properly heat it. It was to prove itself an ice-house.

Perhaps I am better in old houses. Thalassa and the bungle were new, whilst Poona (1892) started my literary career, and I felt it help me.

Maybe I need a solid background.

That early evening along came the landlord who lived in the other part of the house, and he brought with him a huge bouquet of the most lovely flowers from his garden, and a bottle of port. The port was to give me sustenance after the strain of moving operations, and was indeed a kindly thought. I tried to conceal from him that I was T.T.

During the pleasant conversation he told us that my half of the house was haunted. I suppose that this would have been considerably more alarming if I had not already had a hint of it when I saw myself coming down those stairs. I did think that the house might have funny habits, but pulled myself together. Casually I enquired, what was it that was supposed to haunt it? He said that he had seen nothing himself, he was not that sort of person, but he understood that it was an animal which had a nasty look in its eyes! One found it standing beside the bed. 'Which room?' I enquired. It was the one that I had given over to being the spare room, and privately I thanked God for that.

Naturally neither my brother nor myself was too pleased about this, though my brother thought it might be the land-lord's idea of a joke. There were, however, so many other things happening all at once that the joke disappeared into the limbo of lost things. For the time being I forgot the ghost.

I had finished the move, and now I went off on my first journey to Scotland, to visit the *Royal Oak*. She was there, getting herself furbished up to come south to act as guardship for Cowes Week. I went to stay at the charming little inn at Queensferry.

'Don't go for the uniform, it wears out,' said my brother, which was a typically fraternal remark.

Off I went, and after two days up there, when I was having a delightful time, my brother sent me a telegram telling me that during the night Doris had had a small daughter. That baby was one of the biggest surprises of my life, for none of us had had any idea that a baby was coming, which went for Doris too. By the guidance of that merciful providence which shapes our ends, I had asked her old mother to come to be with her while I was away. The niceties must be observed, and my brother *was* unmarried! I rushed home. Apparently there was chaos at Harlow for the moment, and they needed me back there.

I burst into the Dower House on a very cold summer's day and instantly heard the baby crying upstairs. I went up to her, and brought her down to the only fire we had in the house, which was in the kitchen. As I came downstairs (in the blue dress I had worn when I saw myself!) I thought *I have done this before!* It had happened the day I took the Dower House.

This isn't possible to explain. Did I originally step for a second into the future, or what happened to me? I believe this happens to others, and the curious fact is that it signifies nothing at all, and therefore is never worth recording. It signifies absolutely nothing.

The moment they were fit, Doris and the baby went back to Frinton where her husband was, and that was when I found Rose—bless her heart!

Her young man, Jim, brought her over to interview me, and we all liked one another from the start. Rose became part of the family when she said she would come to the Dower House. I have never forgotten the night when she arrived, and I said, 'Cook what you feel safest with for dinner, and just find your feet. Don't bother about us.' She sent in the loveliest meal.

I shall never forget also the sense of someone really helping that she gave me. Her facility in making Pip wash his neck. I shall never stop being grateful for Rose.

I went to Cowes, and on to Sheerness, and there in the Engineer Captain's cabin Robbie asked me to marry him. I have never been quite sure why I said yes (I had intended to say no), but one of those impulses got me, and there we were. I had turned down a string of far more eligible young gentlemen and then suddenly said yes to a penniless N.O. He was entirely unsophisticated (but did not know it). He had done well at school, was the good-boy type and could not tell a lie, which might at times be awkward for me!

'You've gone barmy,' said my brother simply.

Robbie thought that I was a simple child, one of those dear little things, pretty as they come, and all I needed was a gallant male to prop me up. So he was prepared to prop. He's still propping, thank goodness. I knew that he would be dead reliable, awfully punctual, and bang on the beam.

By nature we were as the poles apart, but I did not know it then. He helped me valiantly. He was good at figures and put my passbook straight for me. I can't count. I have jitters and because of this get terrified lest I overdraw. My counterfoil arithmetic being wobbly, and always—so it seems—in the wrong direction, I had solved the worry for myself by every few weeks taking off five or ten pounds so that I was sure that I was on the right side. The bank manager (a personal friend) was narrow-minded about this, I must say. When I explained the simple arrangement to Robbie, he said, 'What a sweet kid you are!' (He was at *that* stage in the proceedings!)

We became engaged, and ten days later he came for a long week-end to Harlow. Will my home ever stand up to the Old Parsonage at Otford? I wondered with some trepidation, for I knew that the Old Parsonage was something of a show-piece. Anyway, now was the chance to try out the supposed-to-be-haunted spare room. I did not think that Robbie was the sort of man who would see ghosts, so we put him in there with a few choice flowers to make it seem friendly. The assumption was that if he said it wasn't nice, then we should realise that there was something funny about it. He said nothing. I think nothing happened. No animal with a nasty look in its eyes, nothing at all. The only thing that he complained about was that my young son took him in early-morning tea and lovingly touched his cheek, then said, 'Sir, you have pins in your face!' Pip had never seen a man unshaved before.

'Let's forget that ghost. I think the landlord did it for fun,' said my brother. I never saw anything all the time I was there.

I did not think that Robbie was impressed by the house (he

should have seen Storyette! I thought), but the Old Parsonage was of course so much better.

He met my father, and we planned to marry in December when the ship came down from the north for Christmas leave. I had as yet to find out the curious habits of the Royal Navy, for the Admiralty was extraordinarily inexact. They said one thing and meant another, I discovered.

I got busy trousseau-making, getting the book I was working on finished and complete, and then the ship came south, much earlier than anyone had expected. I was having heartrending difficulties trying to heat the Dower House, which was a veritable ice box. I bought oil stoves and stood them everywhere, but one would never have known they were there. Gas fires did little. We just could not use the drawing-room at this time of year because it was so bitter.

That was when Robbie wanted to get married in late November, and it was to be at eight in the morning, at the church across the square. You cannot believe how much went wrong! First of all the church was not licensed for weddings, and there was more than a little difficulty in putting this straight. Next, we found that the incumbent was stone deaf, and did everything by lip-reading. He did it magnificently, never dropping a brick, but it was rather a shock to a nervous bride.

I met Robbie in London the night before. We were to have tea together at the Great Eastern Hotel, but an old love of mine would come too, and that spoilt everything. I do think a bride might be left alone with tomorrow's bridegroom, even at the Great Eastern Hotel. Robbie came down to Harlow, supped with us, and this night he did *not* occupy the haunted room, but went to a little inn near the station, where the landlord offered him a brandy with his early-morning tea! Kind, I thought, though hardly a gracious compliment to me!

In the Dower House I was busily changing the initialled linen. I am a great initialler, and had all the D-C.s changed to G.R.s. He noticed it, oh joy! and said, 'Do you know you have my initials on the towels?'

'All of them,' I told him, and he saw that the breakfast cloth and napkins had the same initials.

'I say, this *is* something!' said he.

It was a snow-infested world and icily cold as only Harlow can be. Harlow and Letchworth are the coldest places I have lived in, with Walton third on the list. We ate eggs and bacon over the fire, and went for a walk in the snow, which was a great mistake. That afternoon we had a wedding tea party and someone brought with him a record of the wedding march which he put on the gramophone, to my horror. I thought we should never escape it.

But home is not the right place for a honeymoon, for one can never stop the house from trespassing. The cockatoo should have been a house dog, not a cockatoo at all, and he screamed half the night with rage. Next day Robbie and I bolted to the Great Eastern for a honeymoon away. I realise that the Great Eastern Hotel hardly sounds romantic, but it is extremely comfortable and has the loveliest blackcurrant jam for breakfast, which, as far as I am concerned, covers everything.

Maybe there are moments in one's life when home is no longer sweet home.

Winter was a menace in the Dower House. I had never known that walls could be so thin, it was like being in a refrigerator. I have always felt the cold badly, inherited from my mother, who during the winter lived on hot water and lemon juice, saying it was the only thing that warmed her. That was how she nearly died of anaemia. I had got those smelly oil heaters everywhere, and all the other ideas for heating which always seem to do the job for other people but do nothing for me. We had two big halls, and a large landing. The attics were not shut off, which was a difficulty, and the wind came howling down the stairs. Curtains at the top did exactly nothing, but blow about.

Robbie was horrified by the cold there, and he had just come down from the north of Scotland. It was his idea that in January I should join the ship at Gibraltar. We could have a suite in a hotel he knew there, and maybe go on to Malta later, and get real sunshine. I had never been abroad, of course. I felt a bit hesitant to mention this, because people had been surprised that I knew nothing of other countries, and condemned my lack of knowledge as ignorance.

The thought of warmth was a tremendous push, I must say.

Robbie was the one who thought that felt packing round the leaky windows would help to keep out the cold, and he got the stuff and put it in place with my brother. It did nothing. Whitchurch had been bad, we had dreaded the moment when we went upstairs to undress, but Harlow was a thousand times worse.

The ship would sail in January to join the Mediterranean Fleet, and Robbie would not be home for three whole years. This was the sort of amiable little wedding gift that my Lords of the Admiralty kept up their sleeves for one, and then were surprised that one preferred life with the Army. Robbie said that he felt I ought not to spend the rest of the winter in Harlow, it was too cold. Locally the shopkeepers told me that others had found the house much too cold and had left because of it. It would have been a help if I had known this before. However, I was getting out of it *pro tem*. I had a ticket for Gibraltar in my bag.

'Don't go to a bull-fight,' said my brother, 'you'll only be sick.'

Hotel Cecil
Gibraltar

I thought that I knew something about the sea, but the minute
S.S. *Osterley* turned the corner into the sea past Sheerness I
found that I knew exactly nothing. Nothing that mattered, anyway. The food was lovely, but I was too ill to eat it. It was
cold, for these ships travelling to the heat were never fully
heated on the outgoing journey.

They told me we should be in sight of Gibraltar at six on the
morning of the fourth day, and up I got. They seemed to be
surprised to see me wandering about the deck, for they were
swabbing down. It was a dream morning with a light azure mist
on the shore, and Tarifa looking like a little town of shimmering
pearls beside the water's edge. Behind it rose the mountains in
ice-blue, and when the sun appeared the heat was heavenly. It
was June in January. It was heaven in my life. Gib was in a haze.
Then it appeared, far higher than I had believed possible, and
much further away. I did not miss a single moment of the
approach, not even for breakfast. I saw my first palm tree,
motionless on the shore, I smelt that faint smell of the East, of
musty hide, swarthy Spaniardo, cheroot and Spanish wine, all
in one. We came into the bay and stopped, for we were flying
the yellow quarantine flag.

Already I was learning about ships.

After a while we moved in to the far end of the bay where
the Commercial Mole lay. As we moved, the engines making

hardly any noise at all, the blue water became alive with vivid boats in emerald and sapphire, carrying fruit, some with trinkets and finery, one with caged birds, and all manner of souvenirs. These were the little marketing boats coming off to trade. A Tunisian in a long cloak and fez dangled leather ware at us. The bay had become a bargain basement of curious-looking people.

Robbie appeared in a picket boat and swarmed up the side in a remarkable manner which gave me the jitters. Gangways seemed to offer no difficulties to men. I said the journey had been fine, but he shattered me by saying they had the weather reports and knew it had been dreadful. The worry with the R.N. is that it always knows, with a bit more for luck. I had not realised that most of them were seasick themselves, and had no idea that naval uniform did not mean that you couldn't be sick. I thought the two went together.

'You'd better think again!' said Robbie.

Going ashore was heaven. It was a very hot sun. I shall have to get rid of this coat, I thought, always a joyful experience. The smell of the East intensified, and now there was the strident discord of salesmen's voices, the chatter of mules' feet, *carrozzi* bells, and music. We got into a *carrozzi*, which was like a half-tester bed, and we shot off along an avenue of creamy oleanders into Main Street. The warmth was such a delight; the scent of heliotropes and freesias from the flower market, and then the sight of dangling kimonos and Spanish shawls outside the Indian shops. This, I told myself, is the liveliest springtime of my whole life.

Into the Hotel Cecil we went. This was furnished in lacquered woodwork, bright tawdry scarlet and gold, and very Spanish. No carpets covered the mosaic floors, fans purred, so that everything was most unreal to me. It was like a brand-new picture-book of which I was turning the leaves. We took the lift.

The suite reserved for us was simple. Big double doors opened on to the ante-room, and beyond lay a room painted in soft pink. There were no ornaments. Through the windows I saw two fleets at anchor in the bay, and behind them the hya-

H

cinth mountains of Andalusia. Life is lovely, I am in love with it, I told myself.

The black-eyed maid, Maria appeared. '*Agua caliente?*'

'That's hot water,' said Robbie.

I had spied the small iron balcony with a blossoming wistaria in great big bunches of mauve on it. Below was a courtyard with crimson bougainvillaea everywhere, and a young Spaniard in tight cotton trousers who looked at me. He patted his very black hair and bowed profusely.

'Pewtifuls!' said he, indicating *my* hair. That was how I found they liked fair hair in the land of the matador. He brought out a guitar, they all seem to have this sort of thing somewhere about the person, and began to strum on it, singing in a light falsetto voice.

'What's he doing that for?' I asked Robbie.

'Money, probably. You'll have to watch out, for he likes the look of your hair.'

My trouble in life is that I find it hard to watch out when I should. I get led away. I was already much attracted to a new mode of life. This balcony is going to be a lot of fun, I thought, we don't have things like this at Harlow, nor do we have blue mountains, and hot sunshine in January, and then once again, I simply *must* get rid of this coat.

We lived on the roof garden unless it was too hot, and even in February it could be too hot there. Delicious teas were brought to us by dark men who purred whenever I came into view. The Spaniard likes to show his appreciation, and misses nothing in a skirt. I may be silly, but it *is* gratifying. One feels life is worth while, one is wanted, admired. I liked it.

Presently the local journalists heard that I was there and they arrived. Most of them were Rock Scorps (the rude name for Gibraltarians), and they suggested that whilst my husband was busy in the *Royal Oak* they would show me the sights of Gibraltar, and all the wonders of the Rock. I was now avid to see them, but my husband thought the escort was perhaps a mistake. I might be a sweet kid, but these men knew too much.

Living there was utterly divine, I wrote happily in my diary.

Whilst it was hot one lay in that airy soft pink room with the fans whirling, and the gentle air coming through it. We dined downstairs in the restaurant, and I adored it. We always had Moorish chicken, that everlasting Moorish chicken, and for the first time in my life I learnt that salad (which I had always thought to be quite harmless) could be dangerous. Everyone drank a sweet white wine, that was everyone but myself, and there were the eternal oranges, of all kinds. I was so stupid that I had thought that apples were the only fruit with different names, and had never known that there are all sorts of oranges as well.

I was in love with Spain, not only the warmth of the climate and the gentleness of it, but the warmth of the people whom I met, and I wanted to stay there for ever. What more did I want than a pink room, with Maria coming round the corner, and prepared to do anything in the world for me? One did not buy a bunch of violets, but a dozen every time. Roses by the fifties. Armfuls of freesias and lilies. Why did I never find this place before? I asked myself.

The walls of this home were kind, and I loved the roof garden, the chaise longue, and the thrill of living in an enchanting new world.

We drove into La Linea, passing the most heavily armed guard. We went to mountain villages, walled like the fairy-tale ones, with golden eagles soaring above, and flowers everywhere. Or we had a picnic in the cork woods, which smell of the nicest coffee, and where the cuckoo sings. The cuckoo was passing through on its way to England, and having a short rest. Why doesn't the silly bird stay here for eternity? I asked myself. Returning that summer in August with the Rock hard and grey with dust, and so hot that one wonders how one can breathe and prays for the moment when the sun goes down, I knew why the cuckoo does not stay.

'This is heavenly,' I said.

The ship obligingly cashed my cheques, and whenever I got

stuck sailors came to my rescue. Marrying a paymaster has
something to be said for it, for, as he explained, not only has
he got a comfortable office on board in which one can sit with
him but he has to know all the rag-tag and bobtail of the
place.

There was the Maltese messman, our Mr. Vella, who could
get one any item in the shops for half the price. All one had to
do was to note, say, a coffee service in the window and say this
was what was required. I found that one could spend hours
bargaining with a couple of Indians in charge, trying to beat
them down, and get practically nowhere. One started with a
tenner, and at the end of two hours was down to only seven, and
becoming worn out. Of course, that was what they intended. I
always came away defeated, and then I found that Mr. Vella
was the answer. 'Show me' was what he directed, and off we
went back to the shop, with all those shawls and kimonos
dangling in the wind, and I should have thought rotting in the
bright sunshine. Within twenty-four hours the coffee service
appeared in the pink bedroom, and the bill for £4 10s. with it.
Just my cup of tea!

They were the world's most fascinating shops. All those
tortoiseshell brushes in elaborate cases lined with ruched pink
silk. They always put their money on ruched pink silk, but
somehow I did not think they would fit in with the bedroom at
Harlow. The glittering kimonos, the leather work and the paper-
thin china, besides unending statues of matadors and bulls and
picadors, and all the rest of them.

In the market where I always went to buy flowers for the
pink room I could buy more freesias for sixpence than I should
have thought humanly possible, and then get a large bunch of
violets given me for being so nice. Then, alas, I learnt that they
did this only when the customer had overpaid, just to show that
he had been 'done', I suppose.

To a woman who adored flowers, Gibraltar had everything
in this world. The tall airy rooms, the eternal sound of singing,
and always the flowers. I, who had been brought up in pastoral

villages with the thatched houses and sunflowers, was ashamed to realise that I had found something so much nicer. Give me Spain any day!

But Robbie knew better.

He told me in the siesta hour, with drawn blinds and fans purring and even the flowers in the room fading. There had just arrived a huge bunch of tender pink roses, quite the most magnificent that I had ever seen, and addressed to Mrs. Robinson with the number of the suite. Maria appeared with it, smiled as she gave it to me, and laid a finger on her lips with an artful look in her very dark eyes. 'From the señor,' said Maria.

Robbie was half asleep on the bed as I opened the tissue paper. The flowers were the exact colour of the walls, in the best possible taste. Robbie opened half an eye. 'And where did those come from?' said he.

I hadn't got a clue. Then I found the card and they were from our Mr. Vella. 'Bless his heart!' said I affectionately. Robbie started up.

'Let's see that,' said he, and I handed it to him. He turned slightly red. 'Cheek!' said he, 'and they'll have to go back. He's trying to bribe us. We don't accept anything like that *if* you please.'

Robbie was mess secretary, and could not be bribed. I, of course, would have accepted anything like that, and from any-one, and not have bothered myself too much as to whether it was cheek or not. Why should I? So, after all, the soft tender pink roses never matched my bedroom.

It is a strange thing how that suite, entirely different from anything that I had ever known before, became home and never was anything else. It was actually me. Even on those nights when the levanter came and rattled the shutters till they lost their buttons and started to flap and bang against the wall; even on the nights when it was too hot to sleep; even in any circum-stances. Wherever we went we always came back here. Some-how it was welcoming in its own way. Receiving, I felt. Kind to us. It is difficult to explain how some places are kind to one and some are not, but this is something one feels and knows deep down inside oneself.

I had to admit that I found the Spaniards far more thrilling than the naval officers whom I met, though I always adored 'snotties'. A white patch meant (to me) that its owner hadn't had his brains stamped too much to pattern and could still think for himself.

'Their brains are about your age,' said my husband, but a trifle wearily. He still fostered the idea that I was a simple child, a little girl playing at life who knew nothing that she was not supposed to know. What a little pet! I have always wondered how he got that idea of a journalist working hard in Fleet Street, where you are not paid to be ignorant of life but to know what you are doing.

I decided that Spain was cruel and utterly ruthless, but in spite of the abysmal poverty and distress it had a radiant form of gaiety such as I had never met before. It had the quality of warmth which made me feel they were more alive than we were. And every Spaniard knows one phrase in English, and it is I-love-you. Oh I admit that they know I-hate-you too, but they did not hate me. Spain gave me a lovely sense of personal freedom which is difficult to explain. It was so gay. I could almost stick a red rose in my mouth and swirl a Spanish shawl round me and feel that I had something of Spain in me, a land to dance in, a land to laugh in, a land to love in. I adored it.

We went to the top of the Rock. Everybody does this once in a lifetime, but nobody does it twice, for it is too much like hard work. Mr. Vella provided sandwiches, and off we started before the sun was really high, for the journey takes quite a time.

The upper half of the Rock is surrounded by tremendous iron fencing which is known as the 'Unclimbable Fence', which it is not, for a vigorous young snottie did climb it once for a 'dare'. I came to the conclusion that midshipmen could get anywhere they wanted, and more so if it was forbidden.

We went in at the top of Windmill Hill, presenting our

passes, for there is a great deal of fuss about getting on to the Rock, and we had not gone very far before we met the apes. The mistake is to feed them, for then, when your larder runs out, they get furious, and attack. They can be vicious. We went round to the back of the Rock above Catalan Bay, and then started going up the steps. Very soon we were far above the mimosa bushes and the eucalyptus, and the whole world seemed to be only steps. There were literally hundreds of them. It grew considerably colder, and when it came to eating the sandwiches we had to shelter under some boulders. Deep down below us the boats looked like mere pin-points on a map. Ceuta was quite clear, and superbly azure.

I was getting very worried as we approached the actual top, because I have a dud ankle, most of which I have lost to different surgeons, and I was not at all sure whether it was going to hold out. I had not told Robbie about it. If I had, it was quite likely that he would not have let me try it, and I prefer to try something and fail rather than not get at it at all. Gradually we came to the last eight steps, after all those hundreds. Eight only! Could I believe it?

'Now take in a deep breath and wait for it!' directed Robbie. I did.

What I had not expected was that fierce cold blast which comes in a roaring gale over the top of the Rock. Somebody might have warned me. It had been calm enough climbing up till we got about halfway, but nothing had suggested the tornado on top, and as I clung teetering to a bit of rock I wondered where on earth I should land if I were blown off the top.

We didn't stay there very long.

We came down a great deal faster than we had gone up, and then I went lame. It was middle afternoon when we got to the gate with a waiting *carrozzi* which bowled us back to the hotel. It was siesta time and naturally nobody was about. How amiable and warmly comfortable the room seemed to be, and how sweetly the flowers smelt! I slumped down on the bed and went fast asleep, gradually waking to hear a guitar playing in the distance and knowing by the sound that the *amorata* had begun. Mind you, it very seldom ceases, it is one of those things which are always there, and ready to bob out on you.

I could not believe that I had actually been to the top of the Rock and back. I had returned in time for the siesta, for nobody starts really living till the evening. Shutters are closed, blinds drawn (the Spaniards adore a good fug), and the Moors turn into what the Spaniards call their 'room for pray'. Everyone, especially if they have no home, slips into a side alley and sprawls out on the stones, or against a convenient wall which offers itself, regardless of what goes on around them.

There they bask in refreshing sleep, to wake as I did with the 'bell for pray', and the first enquiring voice of some lover's guitar, meaning that life has begun again.

Robbie woke much later. I had had time to investigate the man in what they called the patio, but which looked very much like the backyard, even of 41 Shottery Road. He blew me abandoned kisses. He was a slender gentleman in shabby trousers stroking the strings of that curious instrument which he played. Then he bowed low.

'Señorita,' said he flatteringly.

'Señora,' said I with dignity, and drew the shutters.

I wondered what sort of thumbprint this place would leave on me, and somehow it did not seem to fit in with the rectory or the cabbage patch behind 41, or Thornlea, and certainly *not* with Thalassa. But I fit in here better than I have fitted in anywhere else, I told myself, and what an extraordinary thing it is!

There was a big dance given on board and I was asked to it. I had gone along to Gieve's shop and had made them send Robbie a boat cloak as a little gift for this, for I had found that he had not got one, and I rather like them. The delight of shopping with Messrs. Gieve's is (a) they trust you, which is important, and (b) they always gently guide you into buying the right thing. I was very new to the R.N. and I needed this guiding.

The dance was heaven. We set off in a picket boat from Ragged Staff steps, in the most brilliant moonlight that I had ever seen. It was an unreal world, something of a musical-comedy world, one felt, the ship beautifully illuminated, and the Marine band doing its best, which was most other people's worst, I should have thought, but it takes all sorts to make a world.

The bother was that Robbie did not dance. I had always danced, and could not believe that this was possible when he first told me. He could play the piano and keep time, but had no idea of moving in time. He just did not understand beat. Music did not inspire him to move with it, and he had to be lumped about, which is *not* dancing. On the other hand, I was a very good dancer; I had won competitions in the period when Moon's, Murray's and the Grafton Galleries held these, and therefore his indifference to what had been very much part of my life was rather startling.

'But,' said his paymaster sub, a lad with extremely bright eyes, 'he has the most efficient junior officers,' which, of course, *was* an idea!

It was difficult to give up dancing when it was almost second nature to me, and something I have missed quite tragically, even more so when stationed in a country where dancing was everything, and to dance the tango with a Spaniard had its own brand of progressive surprises.

The moon had set when we came back across the water, and I was tired. 'You don't think you could learn to dance?' I asked Robbie rather timidly.

He proudly arranged the new boat cloak about his person. 'I could try,' he said.

I'm afraid trying was insufficient. He just did not ever understand beat. We went back to the hotel. Here it didn't matter what hours you kept, for nobody disturbed your slumbers, and there seemed nothing to do save be happy. Surely that is the greatest thing in life! Oh, what an adorable place!

I loved that soft pink room, and beyond it Andalusia, the

eternal sound of music, and *carrozzi* bells, and the lovely feeling that perhaps nothing mattered really.

As spring progressed there came the pre-Lent fiestas, when we went into La Linea, where everyone was romping in the streets, masked, tittering, and gay. There was the soft balminess in the air, the clipping of castanets which are never very far away, and the masks which do make life much much more thrilling. As one walked about a swarthy hand touched the arm.

'You come with me to the bull-fight, *si?*'

'I don't like bull-fights. I'm English.'

'But they are much exciting. You come?'

'And be sick? Not on your life!'

'You are so pewtifuls.'

'Also I am married.'

'One man is most fortunate.'

'Yes, isn't he?' and I passed on.

There was something enthralling about the chatter and the twitter of it. They laugh out there save in the hour of the siesta, and if you wish to preserve your life never never disturb the hour of the siesta. That is rank heresy. Sleep till midday if you wish, none will think you lazy. Why eat that silly breakfast which all the English eat and none of the Spaniards touch? Have a green fig and be happy!

We were to travel to and fro for the next four years, and always to the same suite; Maria was ever enchanted to meet us with a few flowers of appreciation, and ever gay. In Spain one does not become part of a house as one does in England, somehow that is not possible. All the walls are much higher, the ceilings further away, but one is ever enchanted to return to the warmth, that balminess which is Spain, the sound of a guitar and the certain unmistakable look in the very dark eyes.

I believe that I needed all that at the time, for the Dower House was behind me, and although I went back there at times, it was not a place that I loved.

For me the system of here-today-and-gone-tomorrow is not

a good one, but if you marry a naval officer this is what happens.
I knew that Gibraltar would always be my pet place, with the
tinkle of bells, and the smell of hot Spaniard and flowers (though
not always a pleasant association, but ever with one).

Then quite suddenly the ship was ordered to Malta. Here we
go! said I. The Hotel Cecil had made me gay.

Great Britain Hotel
Valetta, Malta

Robbie rushed into the pink room with a wad of notes in one hand and dumped them down on the bed, with 'We're off to Malta. Cook's will help you get there, direct boat is the easiest way, and I've fixed up at the Great Britain Hotel.'

'Good!' said I, but my knees were weak.

'Pack the big stuff right now. A couple of sailors will be here for it in half an hour, and I'll take it with me.'

'Pack the big stuff . . .?'

It was on that day in the room which I adored when I realised the sinister meaning of the words 'Over the hills and far away'. I packed at speed, and the sailors arrived for it, whilst I was left with a small suitcase sufficient to carry me through to Malta, and not for the world would I have let Robbie know that I had no idea where Malta was. As a place it had never interested me. Later I went down to the hotel office, where a *soigné* man called Mr. Serruya (they are all called that in Gibraltar) eyed me coldly. I explained what had happened and asked where Malta was. Immediately he had 'the pleasure'. He produced an enormous map and gave me the latitude and longitude, which I found very dull.

'That doesn't mean a thing to me,' I complained.

He then took a pencil and pointed to a mere dot at the tail-end of Italy, a very insignificant dot, and said, 'That, señora, is Malta.'

'It doesn't look much,' I said.

Mr. Serruya explained that it was an island, gave me the population figures and details of the Grand Harbour, and the mean temperature. He said I could go by boat to Toulon and on by train. It was fatiguing. Or cargo boat direct. Or cross to Tunis and then catch the *Knights of Malta*, but it had rats! I decided to go by cargo boat.

The boat carried benzine. Living in the heart of England as I had done, I did not know a thing about cargo boats (or any other boats if it came to that), but I had to get to Malta or bust, so off I sailed. It was small and very dirty, with an old-time captain who never spoke without swearing, and disliked women on board, but his line made him take four to five passengers, blast them! We were tended by a black steward who did not like us much, either. Breakfast was at six with steak and onions, and I only thank the Almighty that we did not get a rough sea or I might have died. We had lunch at eleven, high tea at six, more steak and onions, and it was fairly frightful. Off Tunis we caught fire about three in the morning, and I have never known more of a fuss and to-do. The sea was calm, and we were so near the shore that surely one could have swum for it? but I had to admit that the benzine was something of a proposition. 'Things that go pop in the night!' said the third officer. Next evening we steamed into the Grand Harbour, and that was terrific.

Malta at evening is a romantically lovely spot. The Barracca rises above the Grand Harbour, and here were hundreds of palm trees, the scarlet and crimson flush of bougainvillaea, and figs and oleanders. Bells rang all the time, and nobody seemed to know why. Some said that the penitents rang them, but I never found this out. The *guido* from the Great Britain arrived alongside in a boat and took complete command. I had never met a foreign *guido*, because we did not have them in Gib, but Toni knew the lot, and he handed me about as though I were a parcel, and I was in the mood which preferred to be a parcel. We went ashore to the Customs House steps, where a huge car waited, and I was driven up what seemed to be the side of a house. We crossed what was then Strada Reale, all stir and bustle at nine o'clock at night, and apparently just the hour for fun.

'Madam is tired, but food is prepare,' said the *guido*.

I entered the very ordinary entrance of the Great Britain to find that the owner and manager was an ex-P. and O. steward, and he ran the place just like the rectory in 1900. We had a suite on the second floor. There were stone floors everywhere to minimise the heat, windows set in Moorish arches, for once the place had been a monastery, whilst below those windows sprawled Strada Mezzodi.

Food was indeed 'prepare', and it was good.

'Madam wish the bath?' asked the *guido*, who knew the lot, and he turned it on for me.

'I'm awfully tired,' I said.

'Yes, yes. I unpack perhaps?'

'No!' said I.

He looked reproachful. 'Tomorrow your husband and the great big *Royal Oak* come into harbour. Tomorrow we see the island, yes? The Hypogeum, Hagiar Kim, St. Paul's Bay, Citta Vecchia, yes?'

'I've seen quite enough for now,' I explained, for all I wanted was to go to bed.

I woke to find brilliant sunshine floating through the pale green curtains, and hear the clash of bells, and goodness me, how those bells clashed! I had the feeling that here I was in a brave new world which I had never even thought of. One appreciates a world which always produces grapes and prickly pears for breakfast. Ginni was my maid, otherwise there were male chambermaids (one gets used to them). Flowers arrived in garlands. I could go down to meals in the dining-room (the chef had first- and second-class diplomas, said they proudly).

I was to come and go here quite a lot during the next few years, and although I did not know it then, this *pied à terre* would always be waiting for me. As my boat dropped anchor in the Grand Harbour I would hear the voice '*Guido* from Great Britain Hotel for Mrs. Robinson', and I would feel at home again. For Malta did that for one. Toni was an adorable *guido*, and throughout the war he wrote to me. He had seen hostilities coming, so had taken the precaution of securing a job in an underground museum, which I thought so wise of him! Don't tell me they haven't got brains!

He and I went out for more flowers to celebrate Robbie's arrival next day. Gin must be ready for him. Scotchy, the teetotal wine waiter, was able to help, he was a veritable Saccone and Speed himself!

'This is going to be nice,' I told myself, sprawled on the mosquito-netted bed, with the fans purring. 'This is a brave new world.'

Most of our time was spent in exploring the island. I had no real friends in the R.N. When Robbie was on board I spent the time working, and then we went out together. I very much wanted to get the atmosphere of the place.

We took long walks round Malta to see everything that the average Englishman does not see. Naturally this gave the worst impression in the ship, for usually Robbie had gone before with other N.O.s, now he came only with me. They resented me. Anyway I was a mess, because I wrote for a living, which was obviously *bourgeoise*, and also I was that lowest form of life, a journalist. The annoying thing was that, very slowly, Miss B. was sneaking up the ladder of success, because even if she *was* careless, even if she couldn't spell, even if she was inclined to rush a job, the girl would and did work. 'It is,' said a commander's imposing wife, all bust and brawn, 'quite the wrong thing in the R.N.'

I was not prepared to apologise for it.

We lived in the happy suite with monastic tendencies, and chambermen. If we did not go to the clubs and entertainments we walked round Malta and I know it like Whitchurch. I admit I got a bit sick of the churches, and it was somewhat of a surprise to find that the life which I had thought would be a round of continuous parties and eternal dancing was spent in seeing chapels and such, trudging over dusty cart-tracks, through crawling grape-vines, and sitting under fetid fig trees panting for a breath of air. I did not even bathe, and I am so keen on swimming, but on my first attempt an octopus appeared, and I do not welcome these as the best companions for a swim.

Now, of course, the whole of the R.N. thought that I wished to live the hermit's life alone, and not join in, which had not been the original idea at all.

I wrote in the long cool room with the soft green curtains until it became too hot, when I lay down for a bit. The atmosphere of the place held me, but I never thought of it as being too friendly. I had the feeling that the ghosts of monks hung about it and did not feel that I was the right person to know.

I became very seriously ill in Malta, an illness from which I have never properly recovered. The ship's doctor fluffed it, for these men attend only males, and they never see to anything serious, for that is popped into hospital. In the end my life was actually saved by a Maltese doctor who spoke hardly any English, and in fact his English was more undecipherable than his Maltese, anyway to me. He was kind, excellent and clever.

I lay in that room watching the shadows sharpen against the white wall of the house opposite; all the houses were white in Malta, whiter than white, if you ask me, and how they hurt the eyes! I lay there wondering if I was going to die. I kept thinking that they would bury me the same day out here, though why that should worry me I don't know. Ginni was attentive, and she kept telling me what lovely funerals they had. If you were rich, and she seemed to think that we were very rich, you could have plaster angels on the hearse. I knew she was thinking about *my* hearse, and that was hardly stimulating! I believe she felt she helped, poor child, because she adored me, and I liked her.

Getting better in those circumstances was a long and arduous business. When I did get better I lay on a chaise longue on the roof garden, all scarlet geraniums and smuts galore, and when

the sun went down we drove round the island to St. Paul's Bay
where it was always much cooler. As July came the vivid green
faded away and the island became all sand and dust, and the
fashionable beige which was the colour of the year in London.
Out here my entire background was beige.

Ultimately my husband arranged for me to come home. I was
too ill to stay on. There was a troopship coming into harbour
and he managed to get a permit for me to sail in her. The
thought of taking this interminable journey and facing that
beastly Bay again paralysed me with fear. This time it was the
Gulf of Lyons which did it, and the Gulf is far worse than the
Bay when it gets nasty. The *guido* bucked me up.

'Madam will be wonderfuls when she see England,' he told
me. The funny thing was that he was dead right.

Then I did something that was absurdly silly. I very much
wanted to give my husband a shantung suit, for he had nothing
but good honest wool. You could hardly call Robbie a dressy
man. A darling, but no good at choosing. I got up one morning
at an hour when I foolishly hoped that the heat would not have
arrived yet. As I tottered out of the swing doors of the Great
Britain, a puff greeted me like cook opening the oven door to see
if the cakes are rising. It did not smell of cake, of course, but of
goat dung, hot horsehide, and Malta, for Malta rejoices in smells
and bells. 'They are the speciality', so the *guido* told me.

I bore with me a woollen jacket which the tailor was to copy,
they would have to send a boy round for the trousers, for at the
moment the jacket was as much as I could manage. I staggered
down Strada Reale. Although I had only a few yards to go, it
might just as well have been a hundred miles, but eventually I
stumbled into the affable little tailor's shop with my jacket.

'Am able in extremes,' said he, meaning God alone knows
what. He could make most pewtifuls, he insisted, and would be
quick and sheap. Very sheap. I appreciated that touch.

He measured the jacket and I was perched on one of those
small black chairs with open wickerwork seats which used to be
in all drapers' shops when I was a very little girl. I thought he

I

would never have done, but at last he handed me back the jacket. 'Pleas',' said he.

The suit would be ready on the day that I was due to sail in the trooper; I told him to send it round to the hotel for me, and there would be a packet with the money in it waiting in the office for him. I wished to pay and he was enchanted at the prospect. I wobbled home again, so worn out that I thought I should never make it, for now the sun was blisteringly hot. Like this I could not imagine how I should ever see Southampton in the trooper, where my brother would meet me in the Lagonda.

The suit arrived the day before I sailed.

Robbie said, 'What's this?' I explained that as he had no proper summer suit for this climate I had had one made for him. You would have thought that he would have been delighted, but he shipped the good old boot face. 'What for?' asked he.

There are moments in life when one wonders why one ever tries! What with boat cloaks and shantung suit and engraved cuff-links, what *does* one do next? Not to mention the plus-four suit despatched from England that winter when he was playing golf and as far as I could see had nothing to play it in.

But I was leaving Malta.

I loved the Great Britain Hotel. I remembered the hour when I had been despairing in that bedroom with returned Mss. from England and had thought: Is it worth it? Why not give up now and admit defeat? Though I knew that the Blooms do not admit defeat. I had gone to the window of the room which was like a chapel window, I had looked down at the street below, with Malts in the shelter of doorways fanning themselves with straw hatchets, and with a tribe of goats waddling along, only too willing to be milked, and the boy calling, '*Haleeb! Haleeb!*'

This was truly the island of romance. This was the inspired island. GO ON, it said. Out clashed those noisy vociferous bells. GO ON, they said.

I went down the Customs House steps knowing that I should return (and I did, many times), and I embarked on that awful trip home, with bad weather and turning into much colder weather. I found myself dreaming of a room with Moorish arches to it, of the bathroom beyond with its enormous bath in which I was lost. 'You must grow big!' the *guido* had told me, explaining that I should find it tricky. Joscelyn was at Southampton to meet me, and goodness me, how it poured!

'Rain! Oh, how beautiful!' I gasped, for I had not seen it for months, and the smell of wet leaves and grass was heaven indeed. 'There is no place like England,' I purred in the admiring voice of a homesick woman.

'It's been raining like this all through the damned summer, said my brother with a curse.

Oh well!

67 Cambridge Mansions
Cambridge Road, Battersea, SW11

In the end the move had to come, of course.

The work was increasing, and if I was to keep my place I should have to be on the spot. Besides, the perishing cold of the winter at Harlow nearly killed. I made the resolution that Christmas Eve, and it was a harrowing Christmas Eve, for I sat in the bath most of the day in a futile attempt to keep warm. First Malta, now this! I thought. I'd be back in Gib very soon, but meanwhile we had *got* to move.

I decided that it ought to be a flat.

I was apprehensive of flat life mainly because I knew nothing about it. We had always had plenty of room, save in Storyette, which hardly counted, but I realised that the rent would be inclusive, which was a comfort. Joscelyn and I went to London and searched madly, going to Battersea because the rents were cheap there. To hell with what they call 'a poor address'! In the end I found a flat to let in Cambridge Road at the same rent as the Dower House, but with no rates, which seemed promising.

The large entrance hall would fulfil the duties of a dining-room too, there were three bedrooms and a comfortable sitting-room, all facing south, which I liked. I thanked God that it had got the sunshine, and so took it. The bother was that I had to move in before I went abroad again, so we should have to get in during the darkest days of the year. What about the dweller on the threshold? I asked myself, recalling Mother's little pal, but there did not seem to be a dweller on that threshold.

I thought I should hate living in a honeycomb, for that was what flat life was, and did I have to know my neighbours or not? A fortnight later the family arrived in Battersea.

The noise was at first unbelievable, for I had ignored the fact that we looked on to the Battersea Bridge Road. Those trams never seemed to stop. Ambulances shot along it, for the Anti-Vivi hospital was the other end of Cambridge Road; and, judging by the fire engines, everyone was always on fire. The one person truly enchanted was Pip, aged nine. As night descended on us, the Duke of Cambridge began its merry business, and he watched people being thrown out, or coming to the gutter to be sick, and thought it intensely absorbing. In the morning the dentist opposite started his work, and sometimes ladies screamed, all of which added enormously to the fun. Why had we never come here before? he asked.

'How do I shop?' I asked Rose. I understood only country shopping, and here was a whirl of shops and streets all alien to me, and I am a rather reserved person when I meet strangers. They scare me. But Battersea is *not* a place of strangers for long, if they like you.

Also it was the era of free gifts. Milkmen arrived from rival firms to hand us free milk (one gave us cream) and small pats of butter. Another provided two eggs for us. The baker came with a free loaf, and a small currant cake, so that we could taste how good his cakes were. Like this, it seemed as if we should live on air. Life was too simple.

When we wanted coal for the kitchener we put a head out of the kitchen window, and called 'Oi!' to the first coal-cart that passed; nothing could have been easier.

We moved in cheerfully, and next day we explored the Battersea shops, and what fun it was! We were living in a world of thieves, we were told, but thieves never foul their own nest. The handcarts were the thing; when somebody had had a successful scoop, maybe a wagon overturned, or there was a raid

on an unsuspecting stall, or a 'do' in the market, round came
the swag. Fat navel oranges at a penny each, once a glut of young
turkeys, and I got a beauty for six shillings. Dates in paper boxes
at fourpence the box. Oh, there was no end to the exciting
bargains that Battersea could offer!

The bus to Fleet Street stopped within twenty yards of my
front door. Life had suddenly ironed out all the problems. Now,
I told myself, I am going to have a real whack at Fleet Street,
and a whack I had!

The flat had no personality, no dweller, and not as much
'feeling' in it as the suites in Gibraltar and Valetta. Usually I
had found in my houses a sense of something which others had
left behind them, particularly in Hertford House and Poona.
This flat gave no trace of any previous owner. I passed closed
doors and had not a clue as to who lived the other side of them,
which at first seemed to me to be absurd, but later I grew accustomed to it. The doors shut like prison doors. But my own bit
of the honeycomb was entirely self-sufficient, and no part of
other people's lives came into it; I did not know who had been
here before me, or if anyone had been born or had died in it. It
just accepted the pattern of other people's living, and did no more.

But it held the latchkey to London. Now, I told myself, if I
am to make the real start, this is the spot. I'll work hard, and in
between trips abroad, oh, how I worked! The flat was an office
to me. It had luck. The sad flop of rejection parcels grew less,
acceptances became more. My brother had gone off to Orping-
ton where he had taken a job, and Rose and I were alone, as
Pip was at boarding school. I took a good look into my own
future.

I had written half a dozen silly light romantic novels, believing them to be the first step into the writing world. That
was a mistake, for their reputation shut doors on me. Oh, how
I have regretted that mistaken beginning! I was not really
romantically inclined, I have little interest in handsome dark
strangers and sweetly innocent little heroines. I wanted real
books. I wanted work.

I met publishers, I met publicity men, and had one of my own. Perhaps they detracted from the home influence of the flat, and home never really came to London with me, but on the other hand at last I was beginning to move upwards. Rose thought that I needed a home, and she was the clever girl who organised it for me. We had Sundays out when the child came back from school. We took picnics to Hampton Court, or Richmond Park, or somewhere where there was real country. The original trip we made was in May, at her suggestion, and I found to my utter horror that for the first time in my life I had not even realised that the buttercups were out. I, who all my life had adored buttercups, had been unaware of them. Laying the big foundation of the career, I had forgotten that at heart I am a countrywoman, inheriting my father's love of nature and fauna and flora, and I had cut off part of my real life.

'It's ever so silly,' said Rose.

She was right.

I loved the flat even if it was not home in the same way. I slipped to and fro between the flat, Spain and Malta, working hard when I came back. It was more detached than any other place I had ever lived in, isolated in a queer way of its own. I began to want to know the neighbours even if they might be nasty; but I never knew them.

I was now appearing in the daily newspapers, doing regular work for the *Mail*, things I should never have thought of doing from Harlow, but I had time here and met the right people. I went to Fleet Street most days, working there; also I had an agent.

I tried to make the new flat part of me, buying new curtains for it, starting fresh colour schemes, and the funny thing was that suites in foreign hotels had changed me, for they now seemed to be home, which Cambridge Mansions was not. Does a home have to be a house, or was it just that this one flat did it for me?

When Robbie's foreign service was up he would come back,

and what would happen then? I could not see him in a flat. Both of us adored gardening, and it was now over a year since I had whipped up a piece of groundsel, or cut a lawn. I was being split into two people, but the writer was taking the lead. I was learning fast, which was what I wanted. I was enjoying myself, too, for flat life is easier to manage, and I was so happy with Rose.

I know now that had I had a couple more years there I should be far further on with my job than I am today. But Robbie came home.

That was the day when the flat was a bower of flowers and damn the expense. I went to meet his train and with trepidation bowled him back, going the long way round down the Albert Bridge Road, so that just at the start he would not see the slums of the Battersea Bridge Road. 'So leafy,' said he, 'very rural.'

That's what he thought!

I wept with joy when he liked the flat. Then, of course, the R.N. presented its little problem on a plate; it has a way of doing this at the most awkward moment it can choose. Robbie, now a paymaster commander, was offered an appointment in H.M.S. *Vernon*, a shore establishment at Portsmouth. One always wants a shore job above all else, but there was one of those little ifs and buts attached. If he accepted this he would have to be prepared to sacrifice a large slice of his foreign-service leave and take up the job in three weeks.

'But that's impossible!' I gasped.

It was not at all impossible with the R.N.

I suppose the flat had been a passing *pied à terre* and I knew when the front door shut on me that it was for the last time. I'd regret its freedom, the close intimacy with Fleet Street, but there was nothing I could do about it. Rose was now married to Jim and when she went it would be for ever. That was a big blow.

'You'll hate leaving it?' Robbie said.

I had a vague forewarning of disaster, for these awful apprehensions always have fun with me. Young girls told me that Portsmouth was exciting, but I was not a young girl any more.

I was in my thirties. Don't go, said a voice inside me, and this had nothing to do with the dweller on the threshold, for we hadn't got one at Cambridge Mansions. I would come up twice a week from Pompey, but the thought did not interest me.

If I had known when the horse van drove the furniture away into store that this was going to be the end of home for quite a while for me I think I should have wept. In the flat I had earned myself something of a name, and maybe I had learnt more about Fleet Street than ever before. It is a street of enchantment, I love the lorries with huge rolls on them, the sound of the presses, and those friends who are always somewhere here and there. It is to me the street of work, and my work is my life.

I do hope that Portsmouth is going to be all right, I told myself. How could it be otherwise? Robbie was home.

The Glenlyon Hotel
Southsea, Hants

The last fortnight in the flat went quickly. I did not realise that an era was passing, for here Rose did everything. I had but to ring a bell for a cup of tea and it came, and soon that 'life of a lady' would be banished for ever. Robbie went on ahead, leaving us to the move, and he planned for us to live at the Glenlyon on Southsea front, which was a hotel that catered for the strange world of naval officers.

'What are the wives like?' I asked.

'Some nice, some nasty,' he said, which seemed to be a fair conclusion.

There was that awful last minute when the van rolled finally up the Cambridge Road with my darling bureau, which once was Great-Aunt Minnie's, sticking out of the back of it, and I had the most dreadful premonition that I was doing the wrong thing. 'I'm going to hate this,' I told Rose.

'Oh no. Not at all. It'll be very nice when you get there,' said she, doling out 'nanny' comfort.

Pip and I went down together by train. Robbie had been under a misapprehension as to the time and place of the train, and we waited in Portsmouth Town station, sitting on the luggage together, for the place was crowded out and there was no free seat. I had now dropped into the darkest despair. To the outer world I am a light-hearted, gay personality, but alone, oh, how I suffer! That hour waiting in the station was one of the most gloomy of my life. *Go back to London,* a voice warned me. *Go right back whilst there is still time, but don't stay here.*

Fey feelings mean nothing, as everyone knows. It would be madness to go away. My husband had got what we knew as a 'cushy job', one I had been angling for him to have for nearly a year now, getting to know the right people in the right way, and here it was. So far our married life had been very much here-today-and-gone-tomorrow, but here we were for three years. *Three years is a prison sentence,* said the something within me. Now I only wish that I had listened to it.

An hour later, scarlet-faced and in a panic, Robbie plunged into Portsmouth Town station panting. There had been a most dreadful muddle (as though I didn't know!) and we bowled off to the Glenlyon. We had an enormous bed-sitter which looked out across Southsea common, with all those prim little avenues of trees, and the brilliant flower-beds under our windows. The scent of wallflowers in spring was something to dream about! Alice was the superior maid in charge, and she had tea ready for us. The Glenlyon was run by 'Aunty' who was a darling fat little pudding, who would do anything in the world for you, but I learnt that she had her indiscreet moments. She was said to have appeared starko in the residents' drawing-room late one night when under the 'fluence. She was helped in her supervision by her brother Tiggy. He printed out the menus most remarkably well, doing this in a small back room of an office, and it took him hours a day. One passed the door, always left open, and saw him sitting there crouched over the menus like some comfortable little dormouse, his shoulders hunched, and squinting at the work with one eye. I must admit that this routine was broken on those riotous occasions when Tiggy nipped out through the back and got loose in the Stag, coming home later in a state of uproar which was most upsetting for Aunty.

Southsea brags of its exhilarating air, but it is *not* bracing, as I found almost immediately, in fact it is so much the other way that I was exhausted by it.

Next day Robbie went off on his bicycle to the *Vernon.* It was then the official method. As soon as I had coped with my morning's work, I took Pip to see the beach which I had promised to do. He was then about eleven. We walked across the green common with the prim little trees, anticipating the supreme moment ahead, when the sands came into view. It would surely be a lovely beach, for the posters had said that.

It was shingle.

'What is this stuff?' Pip asked, he had never seen it before, 'it hurts to walk on.'

There was a jostling bustling crowd, all picnicking or yelling, and we had difficulty in finding a bit of shingle where we could sit down. Side by side we stared before us at the sea, a pier to the right of us, a pier to the left of us, and the island across the water. 'We'll go on the pier?' I suggested.

Walton pier is really a workaday pier for angling contests, and launching the lifeboat, and that sort of thing; Southsea was not. Pip wanted to see the peep-shows, a new venture for him, and naturally the first time he struck the rude one, and I had to explain. I must have been vague, for he kept saying, 'Yes, but what does it *mean?*'

I returned to the Glenlyon, and I sent Rose a postcard which stated baldly, *This is awful*, and I left it at that.

That afternoon we explored the Palmerston Road which had been much puffed-up by the R.N. It was not wildly entertaining, though there was a first-class chocolate shop there which eased my misery slightly. For me a chocolate shop was what the Stag seemed to be to poor Tiggy!

We went to the King's Theatre that night, which was diverting for it was a pre-London show. It was one of those very vulgar farces prevalent at that time, and received by loud guffaws by the R.N. But I am afraid farces have never madly interested me. It would be appalling if now I was thought to be smug, but maybe I looked like it. Robbie told me that on the morrow, Saturday, there was a special show on at the *Vernon*, and I should be expected to turn up and show myself off in best bib and tucker. It would be something of a State visit.

One should never rely on the male member of the family for dress instructions, for the poor dears don't know. Already I had discovered that the clothes I was wearing were not what Southsea wore. I have always had a strong dress instinct, and I realised that usually the N.O.'s wife aheres to the tailor-made suit and the naval brooch in the lapel. I have never worn suits and at that time had not got a naval brooch!

I selected a soft yellow chiffon for this, with a matching hat. In London it was a yellow year, and when I arrived at the gates of the *Vernon* there was everybody in cheap cottons, or suits again. Naturally I stood out in garden-party rig, and it *was* a garden party. Most unfortunately that morning a London paper had published a piece by myself (they had held it at least six months, to choose this awkward moment for it!) on naval ports. It could hardly be a help.

I met some of the wives that afternoon. They were shocked that I had never been inside the Snakery at Valetta. (The Snakery is the Navy's polite name for the women's club there.) Why had I come down here to live? a question I was already asking myself. And why on earth did I write? Wasn't it very embarrassing?

'I haven't found it that way so far,' I confessed.

The literary world is happy and friendly. It does not give a damn why you do this, or that, it happens to be yourself that they wish to know. I had come into a coldly unwelcoming world, and here I was condemned to live for three whole years. It was an eternity. Go, said my heart, go right now! and again I had the hopeless feeling of defeat.

I returned to the Glenlyon in tears.

In a way I was lucky in the hotel arrangements, for the Glenlyon was charming. Within the first month I realised that our periods of time in Gib and Malta when we had known nobody, had perhaps been a mistake. Robbie did not dance, so that I hardly liked to make him go out in the evenings. He was not particularly party-minded, though he was a positive genius at running one. Maybe we should have mingled more.

I was the wife of a 'Pay' in H.M.S. *Vernon*, and of course I should have entertained. I am sure everything would have been better if I had given one big boozy party where people would have found that I was a person, and not just a blank wall. We could hardly do this at the Glenlyon. The cocktail party was now established, the R.N. adored it, but I knew little of it. Dinner for four at a restaurant, or coffee or tea parties, did not fill the blank. I was too ignorant of naval routine to realise any of this, and I dared not take action lest I did the wrong thing. Like this I had no friends. I turned to my work for my friend, and buried myself in it.

The thought of escaping to London (i.e. running away) was still in me, but I am not made of the running-away stuff. Besides, it would have been so awful for Robbie, though of course he might have foreseen this. We took no action. That is the way to lose any battle. Quietly I went into widowhood again. I held back. I worked and did little else. I seldom went down to the sea for the beach was so horrible. I did find a friend in the Isle of Wight, but it was quite a way off. I had not lived in a place where nobody liked me (save at 41) and I was wretched. Maybe one faces antagonism with antagonism, or just draws away. I began to get very bad headaches. The heart was growing bitter so that the energy was sapped out of me. Now I did not want to take any exertion of any kind, for I moped. Life had become too utterly dreary for words, and I pined for Rose.

I stuck to the place and did not run away, which I have regretted all my life, for my enemy was over-armed and too great for me. But I did like the Glenlyon.

The spirit of the place was amiable, for the actual building was kind. There was but one bath to each of the houses (two had been joined together), which meant that frequently one had to wait for it; half an hour could be spent sitting on the lowest stair of the flight behind one, nursing a fat sponge bag and towels. When one did get into it, one dared not take too long, for others beat on the door, or made rude remarks. But I had some friends there, in general the older people, no one of my own age.

I liked stolid Admiral and stout Mrs. Hore, who were always kind. A young surgeon visiting one lunch time dropped an imperial brick with the Admiral, and I was the fool who laughed. (A quick brain is not always helpful.) He met the Admiral in the hall, one of those let's-be-bright young men, and he bounced on to it. 'Good morning, sir. How's Mrs. W.?'

I wonder what I ought to do about all this? I asked myself when Pip returned to school, and I sat in the window staring across Spithead to the island. Leave this damned place, said my common sense, but I did not go.

I loved the view of the island across the water. I supposed that Portsmouth could not help being the place it was; it fitted into a pattern, and the people stationed there had become victims of that pattern, and were not their real selves any more.

It would have been better had we had a car, but we had only Robbie's bicycle. He pedalled off to the *Vernon* in uniform every morning, looking very smart. He did not look so good the morning when he skidded on the tram lines and flopped into a frightful horse bun. Even gold lace is not at its best in that state! I felt privately that there must be something ignominious about entering the *Vernon* like that, and returning salutes with a well horse-bunned sleeve!

I got the idea of hiring a car. It would have to be reasonable, I was not earning a fortune, and Robbie's pay was not all that much, but a car would surely satisfy the starvation for fun? Behind the Glenlyon I found Mr. Savage, who had a huge funeral garage. He owned two magnificent hearses and six mourning coaches. All day these crawled to and fro at funerals and more funerals. But the hour for this sort of performance dies young, by teatime they were free, and that was the time when Robbie came home. I went off and had a chat with Mr. Savage. Funerals were coming and going as we talked. I had always had a morbid distaste for them, but somehow the friendliness of this garage, and the constant flow of them, changed my angle. I became almost funeral-minded.

Mr. Savage arranged for me to have a car, the same one each time, and the same chauffeur, Jim Tier. I have ever been lucky with chauffeurs (I remembered Dulwich), and Jim was a charmer. I did not realise that he was sick to death of crawling behind hearses shipping a boot face, for nobody must ever smile. We could at a moderate cost go out in the early evenings if we wished. I told Robbie what I had arranged.

'You're a funny kid!' said he, still labouring under the absurd belief that I was a kid. Maybe one day the boy would grow up, maybe I had always been grown-up, but we couldn't both be right.

That garage saved my life when I was at my lowest ebb. Round came an enormous car and one could take a picnic anywhere in it. Jim knew the country well, and was one of those men who are ever ready to make themselves useful in any way they can. For the rest of my time there this was how I lived.

Once you get out of Pompey the country is beautiful. The other side of the infernal Portsdown Hills lies life. We could expand. Oh, thank God at last I can get away, I thought.

Twice a week I went to London, catching the breakfast train from Portsmouth Town station, taken there by Jim. I worked all the way up. I worked all the way back. But how ill I felt! In the end I had to see a specialist in London, for my Battersea doctor organised this. My doctor was John Rowland, married to an ex-naval Sister, a Scots girl, always known as 'The Old Dutch'. The Rowlands had been very kind to me.

I remember his telling me that his wife drove him mad singing *Annie Laurie* to the baby at six in the morning. The baby was known as Tookey, a fat bouncing lad, and as John Rowland himself said, 'He looks so succulent that this Christmas we could hardly decide whether to cook Tookey or the turkey.'

He was the most charming man.

'Something is very wrong here,' he said. 'What's happened? Is it Portsmouth?'

'I don't like it. No friends. Nothing to do.'

'Do a bolt?'

'There is my husband; what would he do?'

'Think again, probably,' said he, and then: 'No, look here, like this you'll get damned ill. You don't realise it, but you will. You'd better go and see this chap, maybe he could help.'

He didn't help me, he said the same thing. Never go near Portsmouth again, was his advice. But how could I do this? It might be the only chance for years that Robbie and I could be actually together, and one does not throw aside chances like that. He was worried about the headaches so rapidly increasing. But I am the sort which abides by a conclusion, and I thought, All things end with time, surely?

The summer was the worst time of all, when we sat in that pleasantly amiable room, looking out across the common and the pretty lights came on. They danced round the bandstand. Robbie would nod off to sleep, most N.O.s have a superb faculty for this unflattering habit and can sleep for any length of time. Most of them snore. (Once I had glanced into the mess one afternoon, about two-thirty, to see quite a crowd of baby-faced youths in the early twenties snoring brightly.) I would sit by the window listening to the music and the slur of feet, and long to slip out and dance. With anybody. Anywhere.

But to be young again, to be gay again, to be happy. How desperately I sought happiness!

The band blared out the popular tune of that summer.

> I'm young and healthy,
> So let's be bold?
> In a year or two, or three,
> Maybe we shall be
> Too old!

It said just what I felt as I listened, and cried a little, and felt even more hopeless than before. Portsmouth showed my youth fast slipping from me. I longed for the dancing years at Frinton,

K

and the tune of *Swannee*, with the dawn coming round the far corner of Pole Barn Lane. Inside the Glenlyon the lights were rather dim, and everything was orderly, unless it was one of Tiggy's nights out. In the bandstand on the Common there was the vivid brightness of youth, emotion, and joy, and these things seemed to be going from me.

> In a year or two, or three,
> Maybe we shall be
> Too old!

Three years of it! Three solid years I thought. But there came the end when Robbie was appointed to the 'Mighty *'Ood'*, the biggest ship in the Fleet. She was a Plymouth ship, and he was back at the old routine. Spring cruise with Gib, Scotland when summer died, and the routine of the Atlantic Fleet. I would return to London, to a flat in Battersea perhaps, because I would not swop Battersea for the world. I would get the furniture out of store, and Great-Aunt Minnie's bureau would wobble back again, and Rose would help me move in.

We discussed the future during our Sunday walks in the island. The island provided the nearest real country, for Portsmouth stretched so far through unattractive places with names like Cowplain and Waterlooville, and all the rest of it, that it was quicker to take a boat across the water, and walk in the island. I doubt if either of us realised how much the world was changing. Domestic help was far more difficult to get. Big houses were becoming too expensive, and smaller ones in great demand. I did not mind; Robbie has always longed for some house that is rather lovely, maybe the Old Parsonage did that for him in the early days. I thought the flat again would be the answer, and surely the servant problem could not be that bad?

I went up to London to find a flat, and an agent told me that the Albert Bridge Road in Battersea was the right place for me. It might not get as much sun as Cambridge Mansions, but it had a lovely view. No lorries used this road, and at night you could lie there listening to the owls in the park. So he said.

He had a maisonette at a hundred a year, which he thought was exactly 'me'. He had taken to me in a big way. I went to see a first- and second-floor maisonette, with two sitting-rooms and kitchen, a large bathroom, and three beds, all of them fairly large.

'But what about staff?' I asked.

Glibly he assured me that this would be no bother. I should need a good housekeeper. I must say that the word 'housekeeper' was infinitely preferable to 'cook-general', which was what I had known to date. I admit I was half afraid, but he was a very glib young man. I did not realise that time was moving on fast, and now with so many more jobs for women in the world, the domestic side was suffering badly. Robbie came up to town with me to have a look at the maisonette, to see if he approved, and he did. He liked the balcony, the tall rooms, and the view of the park. I signed the lease, and arranged for the landlord to paper and paint, for those were the good old days when landlords did this. They would rush it through, said the bright-eyed young agent, and added that it would be so nice to have me in the neighbourhood again.

Robbie did not care for him. I was only thinking that Battersea was home, whereas Portsmouth was *not*, and never could be.

'You—you hated it?' he said, as we took the train back to the Glenlyon.

'Very much,' I agreed, then rather sadly, 'I have the most awful headache.'

61 Albert Bridge Road
Battersea, SW11

It was summer when Rose came up to help move in to the new maisonette. I think I have never been so pleased to see anybody in all my life as I was when I opened the door to her. She stood there smiling gaily. 'Well, here we are again, aren't we?' said Rose, and we were!

The furniture vans arrived immediately after her, and the two of us got down to it in a big way. Here, I thought, I should lose my headaches, the depression, and the awful feeling of constant tiredness. John Rowland was not too happy about it. He walked into the move to see us.

'Hello, Rosie-posie!' said he.

We had a talk. I said that having got back to London I could nurse my health, and I'd be sensible.

'That,' said he, 'is always the answer the morning after!' and he sighed. Only last night he and the Old Dutch had had a row. He had taken her off to help him with a case, and somehow or other the car door had not been properly shut, and the Old Dutch had rolled out into the gutter in Cheyne Walk.

'Is she hurt?'

'Oh no, but she's furious with me. I hadn't shut the door properly, I suppose.'

'I expect it was your fault.'

'Everything in life is my fault. That's marriage!'

He gave me a talking-to about the headaches, and my state of health. I knew he wasn't happy.

The new maisonette looked lovely. Even the portrait of my great-aunt, with her smug Victorian ringlets, suède gloves and unforgivably low bodice, looked fine. Rose would stay with me until I got somebody else fixed up, and she would show the new woman the job. Everything went very well—so far.

Robbie appeared for the week-end, and we sat on the balcony listening to the birds singing in the park. He liked it. When he departed back to the *Hood* I interviewed a trail of women, and engaged Mrs. Smith. Rose would show her the 'ways'. Both of us ignored the fact that already the 'ways' were dying the death and this sort of life was ending.

I knew from the first that Rose was not happy about her, but she had been the best of a very varied bunch of women who had answered my advertisement. Rose had said, 'She seems funny to me,' but I had engaged her now. I had also fixed up with a little visiting housemaid, a darling Cockney, with two children of her own. She would have fitted in anywhere, but it was very apparent that Mrs. Smith was not a vast success. She had strange moods. She was not used to managing, and there was only one pudding that she could make—tinned fruit salad!

When I was left alone with her I had a private fit. The maisonette was one of my prettiest homes, with blue shot curtains everywhere, new Indian rugs, and a bathroom of marigolds on pale turquoise. The balcony overlooking the park —and it is an extremely lovely park—was ideal. Mrs. Smith was the hitch, and oh, what a hitch was she! If I dismissed her I should be alone, and I had a woman's magazine wanting a serial. 'Be as quick as you can, it's a rush job,' the editor had said.

I had not realised that you cannot keep on a house if your housekeeper dislikes you, and she did—very much. The place liked me, and I liked it. Our front door was halfway up the stairs, so that the family below got the dweller on the threshold, which was no worry to me, but now I had a vague sense of uneasiness.

I slipped back to Southsea, for I read in the paper that the *Hood* was unexpectedly coming back from Scotland. I read this at the dentist's. The fleet had gone off to Invergordon, and I almost thought that a war must have broken out or something, but here they were romping back to port again. I had a sudden inspiration. I would dash back to Southsea if Aunty could put me up (she could), and be standing in the dockyard when the 'Mighty '*Ood*' came in.

I rushed off to Ninette's for a specially nice dress, and a matching hat to go with it, and down to Pompey I travelled, looking like a duchess. I had now regained some of my courage, and could face the place. I felt stronger. Aunty was enchanted to see me, even Tiggy unhunched himself from the evening menus and smirked amiably. Alice welcomed me, and 'Everleen' was interested.

I went off to the dockyard.

The first thing that struck me on arrival was that everything had changed, which surely could not be true? This was not the dockyard with which I was so familiar. It had always been a rule that if one wore a naval crown brooch (gift of devoted husband to show that one had naval connections), that was sufficient to ward off trouble. Not so now. Dressing like a duchess is not always to the good, and I got chi-iked! I stood quietly at the quayside, by the empty mooring place, and saw the *Hood* come in, and how she did it in that tiny space I shall never know. There could not have been two inches to spare as she came alongside (at one time I had to turn away because I daren't even look at her), but she did it. Soon after that Robbie appeared.

'Why are you here? You should be at Invergordon?' I said.

'Invergordon was the trouble.'

There had been a dreadful time up there, almost a mutiny; in fact I could not see what the difference was. I had never supposed that anything of that kind could happen, nor had the officers. They stood dead loyal, of course, and whatever the men may have thought, the officers' pay was insufficient, and they had no marriage allowance either. Robbie thought that it would be all right now, but it had been a very nasty experience. Neither of us appreciated that this was the thin edge of the wedge, which revealed the future. It could change all our lives. Our attitude was that it was a pity it had ever happened, horrid to live through, but over now.

Robbie and I had the most fascinating week-end, something in which stolen leave always excels. He was kept busy on board all day, of course, but to be back in the Glenlyon was quite a treat with the amazing contradictoriness of such things. It was unfortunate that at the moment's notice she had had Aunty had been able to give us only a back bedroom, which had no sea view. Worse still was the fact that the Salvation Army barracks were opposite, and they practised the most deplorable hymns, it seemed to be both by day and night. When they were not singing they were at cornet solos, and I have never been madly attracted to the cornet solo.

It was a radiant week-end.

We had good weather and we did all the things we had hated doing when we were stationed here, but did them because we always had. Coffee at the Savoy on Sunday, the Mikado for tea, and supper at the little French restaurant, where Robbie made me drink some light wine, which made me laugh. Portsmouth had never been funny before, now it was singularly amusing.

When we got back, Tiggy had had one of his nights out, and the family was in some confusion. One of them stated that he was 'a monster', another said he 'behaved like a beast'. Poor, poor little man, a positive prisoner in that back room where he ground out the menus day after day, and must have got sick to death of them. Surely he deserved his occasional break-away?

Perhaps the R.N. is the sure background for 'Parting is such sweet sorrow'. The *Hood* was off once more, and I was back on the morning train for Waterloo. It had been fun, something I had thought I could never say of Southsea, but this time I had enjoyed it, maybe because I knew I was free of it.

Now what about Mrs. Smith?

The little daily woman greeted me. Her Christian names were

Alice Patricia, and we always knew her as A.P. A.P. came scampering down the stairs to meet me.

'There's been trouble here, madam. Ever such trouble. It's that Mrs. Smith. Tst! Tst! Tst! I thought I'd better warn you. Now give me that bag.'

We went up together into the sitting-room. The place looked so charming, it was quiet, no cornet solos here, and it seemed utterly delightful. A.P. had tea ready for me. She suggested that I had this first, and I did.

Within the next momentous hour it became only too plain that I and Mrs. Smith could never make it together. It was fair on neither of us. I wanted someone who fitted into the house and became part of it, like Rose and dear little A.P. I wanted peace in the home. I got another advertisement going, and sat back to interview applicants. At first there was nobody, oh horror! Then the most peculiar string of them started to arrive. It was quite clear that the old times had gone, and that it was hopeless. A midget was amongst them, she had been a dress-maker (trade name Mme Esmée), and it worried me, for I was sure that the poor thing was desperately hard-up. I gave her something for herself, and that increased the string of applicants of all kinds. The news got round. Several congenital idiots applied. One admitted it.

'I try to please,' she said. 'I can't read, of course, or count, or that, but I try to please.'

This was no good.

A.P. was my great white hope, but she had no willing friend. She would have come herself to live in, but there was her old man and the kids. That, she said airily, skiboshed the lot! It certainly did.

The thought of living here entirely alone with just dailies alarmed me, and I felt that it would be impossible. Rose could not return permanently, of course, and it rather looked as if the Albert Bridge Road maisonette had *Hail and Farewell* as its motto.

Rose appeared for the week-end after Mrs. Smith had gone.

'All this lot are no good to you,' she said.

Robbie was due to go up to Scotland this week-end, and I was stuck with an unworkable maisonette and horror in my heart. He came bolting up to me, and we sat in the very charming sitting-room of the maisonette, and the fact that it was so charming made it all the worse. He wanted me to move into a hotel. This was not working out. The furniture could be returned to store, but I hated the idea, but what can you do when the roof caves in and the four walls come down round about you? This was exactly what was happening to me.

Whilst we were in residence at the Glenlyon last summer we had made friends with a charming old colonel and his wife who were living there. They had mentioned the Onslow Court Hotel in Queen's Gate, where they spent the winter. In fact it would seem that their lives swung between the Onslow Court and the Glenlyon, with occasional visits to friends. They had found that a roof of one's own demanded too much of them today, which was exactly what I was discovering at this very time.

Robbie rang up the hotel, and arranged to go round. He went on to our balcony and whistled up the next taxi, for life in the Albert Bridge Road was as easy as that, and we went round to visit the Onslow Court together.

It stood at the corner of Queen's Gate and the Old Brompton Road, into which the back door opened. Coffins went out that way; I once ignominiously left from it with mumps, and was transferred to an ambulance waiting there, to my disgust. It was a spacious hotel with big lounges where you could lose the people whom you did not wish to meet too often, which is the eternal advantage of hotel life. The staff were quiet and charming. Carter was head porter at the time, and a dear, nobody could have been more helpful. Miss Willatt was the name of the manageress, she and I became great friends later. It was an immense relief to sit down and have tea with no worry.

'I think this is a good bet for your future,' said Robbie.

Maybe it was the end of my sufferings which at the moment were more than I could bear, all housework, domestic rows and complications. The novel on which I was working at the time had gone most desperately wrong on me, which is the natural result of home worries. No writer can afford to have this muddle about him. At the same time I have always hated to part with my personal furniture, a lot of which we have had for generations. I adore the portrait of the Rose of Norfolk, my great-grandmamma. The clock which has chimed the hours for five generations of us. All my clocks have names; Robert is that clock, Gertrude is my girl clock, a French *m'lle*, and Mrs. Smith felt that I was crackers about this, but it so happens that I have a 'thing' about clocks. Maybe Mrs. Smith was right.

'I don't want to part with the things,' I said.

'If you don't part with them you'll have a bad illness, Rowland says so,' said Robbie, 'so pull up your socks!'

Up came the socks!

I had one dire day with the furniture vans, but A.P. was there to assist, and she was a very ready help in trouble. She never got annoyed, or reproachful, and treated most of it as a joke. She would come back later, she said, and do what she could for me at any time, bless her heart. And she did.

When the last van had gone I got into a taxi and said, 'The Onslow Court Hotel, please.' Off we went. What a mistake this had been, what a waste of time and energy and planning!

Maybe one is prepared to suffer to get the right sort of roof, but I'd be better back in hotels, surely, though I had some doubts about the Onslow Court because I am by nature desperately shy. I show my worst side on meeting a stranger, and this hardly makes for happy friendships buzzing all around me. How shall I ever have the courage to go down to dinner alone here? I wondered. We skipped over the Albert Bridge. We shot off towards Queen's Gate.

It has a very good address, I thought.

Onslow Court Hotel
Queen's Gate, SW7

The Onslow Court was very much like others of its kind, save that I am sure it was far nicer. They were so good to me on arrival, and by the end of the evening I had found several new friends. Miss Willatt was always near to see that everything went well.

There was a crowd of old retired people, with pepper-and-salt hair, but my great-aunts had given me a good training for such folk. I understood them better than did most. There was a smattering of the young, and it was lively. It was gay. The circumstances of the times had brought people like myself to this place, because the difficulty of running a home was great. It made living unbearable. The hotel was coming into its own.

Robbie rushed up for one night, and liked it. He was so thankful not to see me for ever fiddling with a duster, or trying to bodge together a meal, whilst Great-Aunt Minnie's bureau was littered with the morning's letters from *Home Notes*, and I kept on panting, 'How shall I *ever* get this done?'

That was quite a restful autumn, and I took it quietly. I was badly needing a rest. Soon afterwards Pip arrived back from school, and we dashed into one of the very best, if not quite the best, Christmases of my life! Miss Willatt was a genius at this!

Early in the week there was the children's party with a crowd of little girls in muslins, and little boys in Etons, all of which discloses the date. They swarmed in in their dozens, and Father

Christmas *did* positively appear. We all joined in to help. There was Robbie with a young stockbroker springing about Queen's Gate, clipping together coconut shells to represent the galloping reindeer of Father Christmas's positive approach! It was remarkably lifelike. They caught the cold of their lives, and everybody passing thought that they were mad, of course, but that was that!

There was the gala fancy-dress ball on Boxing Night. My son had been anxious to go as a Cavalier, why, goodness only knows, but maybe that is the sort of thing a teenager feels to be exciting. It was most unsuitable for him. I coaxed him out of it, and playing up his red hair, organised a Ginger Nut outfit. Most of Boxing Day I sat in my bedroom sewing at an orange tunic for him, and Messrs. Huntley and Palmer had supplied us with all the labels we required, and an enormous tin of ginger nut biscuits with which to keep the pangs of hunger from us. I felt that we should be eating ginger nuts for ever and a day. Pip won first prize that night, and it was a gent's dressing-case; the Onslow Court did have the most magnificent prizes.

Although the fancy-dress ball was fun, I enjoyed the next night even better. I think I laughed more than at any other time in my life, and how I adore a good laugh!

It was the staff party, when everything was reversed. The residents took over the staff jobs, and the staff arrived in plain clothes with their friends, and enjoyed themselves, waited on by the residents. Robbie was a waiter, and in the right rig. Pip became a lift boy, in a chocolate uniform with Onslow Court on the lapels. One of the residents, nice Mr. McPhail, took over Carter's job. He made a most wonderful entrance exactly as the clock struck, wearing the chocolate frock-coat with heavy gold lace stripes round the cuffs, and I must say he was *the* head porter.

Very soon after, some new residents who had booked in that week entered the hotel. I shall always think this booking had been overlooked, for nobody knew a thing about it. They and their luggage appeared at the head porter's desk. Mr. McPhail (dressed as Carter) lifted his eyebrows slightly, but then signed them in in the most superior manner. He wafted them to the lift, calling Pip. 'Page!' said he commandingly, and despatched them to their room. There had been some ghastly mistake, and it was not the room which they had chosen. They were annoyed, and Pip came down again to say so.

'Oh hell!' said Mr. McPhail. He then sent Pip back with the right key to the right room, but he returned to say that they were still raising a dust.

'Take them up a bottle of beer with my compliments,' said Mr. McPhail, 'I'll shove it on my own bill, damn it.'

Pip was giggling. 'Do I say "The hall porter sent you this"? and won't they think it a bit funny?'

'You tell them anything you think they will damn' well swallow,' said Mr. McPhail.

Pip told me afterwards, 'I really don't know what those people thought this place was, but the chap gave me half a crown for getting him some sandwiches, which I pinched from the staff supper, and I'm not saying anything about that one!'

As you can imagine, next morning, when the new residents found Mr. McPhail (no longer head porter) eating his breakfast and reading *The Times*, they must have come to the conclusion that this was a madhouse.

The residents worked hard this particular night. It was about three in the morning when the last guest left, and Robbie was gallantly attempting to cope with the drunks in the cloakroom, and finding this the end of the perfect day. He took our own table waiter outside and set him down under a plane tree on the pavement. He could do no more. Then the last remaining residents turned to and cooked hot sausages and bacon for us all, to round off the evening. Being staff was quite the most exhausting thing.

But, thought I as I dragged myself up to bed, this *is* what Christmas-time always ought to be! What fun it was, and oh, how much I had enjoyed it!

The Onslow Court provided me with no outside work to do,

it was all done for me, so that I could get on with writing and journalism and then sit back and enjoy myself. Very soon I had plenty of friends who were living there, which meant that when I wanted to sit about and talk to people I could do so. It opened a new world for me.

I do not play bridge, and some, I am sure, felt this was a pity, but I have never liked it. They had a pleasant room for it, and I remember Pip being joyously elated because when he was looking through the glass doors to it he had had the luck to see some peppery old Anglo-Indian colonel have a fit there!

'That's what they do in the bridge room!' said he.

One could sit and talk in the evenings, play ping-pong if one wished, or have an occasional rummy party, and it meant that I was never hopelessly alone, which had happened to me too often. I knew now that Robbie had been quite right when he had wanted me to come here to live for a time. He had realised that I needed the companionship of others, and some relief from the penal servitude of Portsmouth, for that was what it had been. I could not be unhappy at the Onslow Court, it was a complete colony, we had our own jokes, our fun, our own scandals. (This was a long time before the horror of John Haigh came to the hotel.)

My health had not improved. The headaches had increased in frequency and strength, and John Rowland was constantly round, and worried about me.

'They're taking hold,' he said. 'I can't think why you stayed in Portsmouth so long.'

'If I had returned to London I should have been alone, and it would have been too expensive.'

'A girl with your looks need never be alone for long. You must have known that.' Then rather pensively he said, 'I wonder £ s. d. worries you; without a doubt you should try blackmail, you'd have done well at it, and I should have thought it far more profitable than journalism!'

He always made me laugh.

Possibly I ought to have run away from Portsmouth Town station when I first got there, only I hadn't. Now it was too late, and of course given time I should be better.

The Onslow Court did something for me with the work. I published a gay little book called *The Log of an N.O.'s Wife*, and this brought me in the most excellent reviews I had ever had; they thrilled me. It ran into several editions. The R.N. was *not* amused. Even worse, they were furious because it was so true. They had behaved atrociously, they had treated me like dirt, and now, unheard of in their honoured ranks, the wife of one of them had proceeded to sweep the floor with them, in no measured terms.

The fact that I dared assert myself was the greatest possible help to me, and a real joy, for it put me back on my own two feet. Suddenly the Admiral's lady could no longer terrify me. It seemed that I had outlived that era. One Saturday-night dance at the Onslow Court a very charming admiral came, and with him his slightly bellicose lady. She had a dart at me. She actually attacked me full belt in a corner of the ballroom, but this time I did not say nothing and shrink away. I did not even say 'yes' and 'no' according to the formula which King Alfred started (probably).

I said, 'Now look here, you are an admiral's lady and I am a common journalist. We both have our jobs, and do them, and if you stick to yours and leave me to mine you'll do far better than throwing your weight about like this.'

I thought she would have a fit, she went a ghastly shade of purple, and the Admiral led her away.

The reviewers had liked the book, it did a lot for me, and was followed shortly afterwards by the novel which established me. It was not light romance. It was something after my own heart, and called *The Gipsy Vans Come Through*.

I got the idea from my own family when my great-grand-mother—the daughter of a 'diddicoy'—left a legacy to all of us who have followed in her footsteps. Each of the family has borne something of her mark, for the ruts of those scarlet and yellow van wheels do come through the generations. I suppose my passionate love of bright colours came from her, my adoration for walking barefoot, and an awful tendency to steal flowers (if you trust me in your garden), all of which are part of the diddicoy heritage.

Walter Hutchinson thought it would be quite an idea to give a big party to start off the book. Publishers used to do this, and the author paid half. I doubt if he ever got his money back, but always hoped for it. The Onslow Court said they would do it for me, and dear Miss Willatt was fascinated and went at it in a big way.

I have never been very good with cocktail parties, which I find noisy and a bore. I always want to sit down, but if you do you look such a fool. I wanted my first book party to be really different and I got busy. With the help of John Rowland I managed to fall in with some real gipsies who were camped on a piece of waste land in Battersea, and who would assist. He knew them, for one night one of them had rung him up asking if he could go to their camp and see Minnie, who was very ill. *Very* ill, he emphasised. Off he went, the Old Dutch refusing to go with him because she did not like gipsies.

When he arrived he found that Minnie was the moke! John explained that this was not really his line of country, and was instantly told that he had been so good with the dad's quinsy that he was the only man they would think of consulting about Minnie! So he dealt with her.

I was taken to visit them, and sitting in a van with their queen made adequate arrangements for a band of them in full dress to come to the Onslow Court on the appointed day, sing their lavender song, and tell fortunes. They were most willing.

The scheme went further, for I had a friend who was assistant stage manager at His Majesty's Theatre, and he wanted to come to the party, so tried to be helpful. They had a gipsy van amongst their props, and he would get this brought along to me 'for free', which he did.

I was a little apprehensive for I had never tried to give my

own wares a boost before, but as a party it went quite magnificently. The gipsies arrived in state. Pip had to fetch them for
me, and came bowling along over Battersea Bridge with them,
and they gave him a few honest-to-God tips in that little delight
which is known as 'Spotting the Lady'! They were a chatty
bunch and I doubt if anyone knew what they were talking about,
but that did not seem to matter.

I had been half afraid that no one would want their fortunes
told at a cocktail party, but there I was utterly wrong. The men
fell for it, even deserting good strong drink to get the future
revealed to them. The lavender song was a charmer. Though
naturally I had hardly meant the gipsies to *sell* their lavender at
the same time, but somehow this got into the picture. 'Just a
little bit for luck, lady,' which was their way of business.

They behaved most beautifully, and looked quite lovely in
their gala dresses, one would have thought that butter could not
melt in their mouths, but there we were wrong. When I had
talked about the party to them I had explained quite strongly
that whatever happened nobody must be short of anything when
the party ended. There must be no nonsense of that kind.

'Pretty lady!' said they, aghast that one so charming could
foster such abysmal ideas of behaviour.

When the party finished nobody had missed so much as a
pin, for they had stuck to their word. When they had done with
us they went down below to the staff rooms and kitchens, to
have some refreshment. Chambermaids, pages and waiters and
porters were all for getting their fortunes told, and I had never
said a thing about nothing being missed from those ranks. I had
not even known that they would go down below. That *was* a
mess!

The book did well. I don't know if a party helps, or if it is
the good reviews, or the prod one puts behind it here and there.
I have never been very good at sucking up for reviews, and
privately felt that the whole party was a colossal sucking-up.
But the sales were good. A writer works hard. This is not a
matter of a few hours, but a few months. Time goes on and on,

L

and the wretched manuscript is still demanding things of him. Much depends on the hour at which it is launched, I suppose, for time has a tremendous influence on the publication. There are wheels within wheels, and every year I should say that it becomes more difficult. Maybe success is the fairy doll on the Christmas tree, not there for the taking, but always reserved for the next time.

There was no doubt about it, this system of living was far kinder to my work, and far less worrying for me. I was not for ever pursued by the dreadful guilt complex of the fact that I ought to be doing something else. Could it be that a roof and four walls could be too demanding of me?

At the same time a hot summer in London can be wilting, I found streets irksome, and longed for a garden which was impossible to get. The sea seemed to be a long way off, and walking by the Thames at Putney did not really make up for it. Perhaps one could not have everything, and I wanted too much? At the same time I felt I could have a little more than I was getting, and what could I do about it?

The answer came through Captain and Mrs. Croker who were staying at the Onslow Court. During the summer they went to live in a country hotel which they adored. Mrs. Croker suggested that perhaps we could do the same thing. It *was* the answer.

When I first mentioned it to Robbie, now working at the Admiralty, he thought it was not a good idea, and dismissed it. A bad heat wave in London changed his tune, and the heat was suffocating. One very hot day I persuaded him to come with me down to Lamorbey Park (it was at Sidcup) to visit the Crokers, then staying there. I suggested we could have tea in the garden, and come home later, and no harm would be done. I don't think he really wanted to come, men being men, but all the same he is a very nice person and he said 'yes', for my sake.

Sidcup is just about twelve miles from Charing Cross, and in those days it was, of course, far more countrified than it is today.

Now they have cut down the elm trees round the station and put up the cheapest form of shops, with the bakelite look which is so dismal. Then it was better.

We walked out of the station, and towards Lamorbey as the Crokers had told us, and we turned in at the gate which was marked LAMORBEY PARK. The old mansion had belonged to the Malcolms, Lily Langtry's family. The grounds spread to 150 acres, taking in the golf-links, two quite large lakes, and even some woodland. We walked along the path for about a quarter of a mile, and saw the house between the trees. We went on and past the walled back garden and turned the corner to the house. Here and there the upper lake flashed through the trees. There came a sudden flush of colour where lupins strayed wildly, or roses bloomed against a wall. Swans shimmered on the water.

As we turned the corner we came to the façade of the house, standing facing the bowling green and the upper lake. On the far bank late rhododendrons blossomed in a profusion of pink and pearl. The place was radiant.

We went inside and saw the important climbing staircase and the strange wind gauge on the wall. Lamorbey Park was one of those places where nobody worried what you did. We were allowed to wander round just as we would. We went down to the lake with the punts on it, past the hard tennis courts, and the grass ones. Past the croquet lawn too.

I got excited. 'We have simply got to come here,' I said.

We had tea together in the garden, and could take the trays where we wished, so we sat under the rose-pearl rhodies and drank it. Then we had a word with Mrs. Musgrove, the manageress.

'How do we manage to stay here?' I asked.

It was not as easy as it seemed.

The place was owned by Mr. Sheppard, known as Bertie; he was managing director of Johnson, Phillips, the cable manufacturers. Bertie was a hard-drinking but very friendly man, and he had his own ideas about the people who stayed there.

At the end of the war he had been drinking in the golf club, at a time when he was living in Blackheath. Lamorbey was empty then, and he was told that someone was buying it and intended to cut down all the trees. He thought it would be a disaster if anyone did that, so he just walked out and bought the place himself.

It must be very nice to be able to do that sort of thing, but these ventures have a way of catching up with one later on. He discovered that Lamorbey was an extravagant luxury, and when he went into the matter further he found that it was slightly large for himself, his wife Alice, and their one daughter. This must have been something of a jar to a man like Bertie, but he got over it by turning it into an hotel. Then the idea tickled his fancy. He was crazy about bowls and snooker. If he chose wisely, he would always be able to get a game of either whenever he wanted it. He warmed to the comfort of the idea.

So he opened up as a hotel, but it was not the ordinary hotel, for Bertie was never an ordinary man. He arranged to have something after the manner of the admirals' interview which can bar one's chances (or the other thing) for the R.N. If Bertie took to you, then you became a Lamorbeyite for ever; if he didn't, then all the money in the world would not get you in. Mind you, he was dead fair. He did not maintain that he must always win, or any nonsense of that sort. To Bertie a game was a game, and you played as best you could. The male guests had to do this, and they had to be exceptionally good to beat Bertie.

He preferred good-looking women about him, undoubtedly he had an eye for women, and let this rove round when it came to his guests. He was married to Alice, who was a darling little pet who adored croquet. I did notice that Bertie never asked if the women applicants played croquet, that did not worry him, and I doubt if he was that much interested in poor little Alice.

The cost of living at Lamorbey was about four pounds a week, for which you got all sorts of games, bathing and boating; Pip could ride the pony if he wished, or borrow a gun for pigeons and rabbits. What more could you ask? It was my idea of a dream come true.

On this our first visit there, we sat on the lawn drinking tea, and deciding that this would be ideal for the summers, just as the Onslow Court filled the bill when winter came. It looked easy enough. Bertie preferred the Navy to the Army, and Robbie did play snooker and bowls. Mrs. Musgrove had taken one quick look at me when I made my first enquiries, and had said, 'You'll do', and I admit that Bertie's piercing eyes brightened considerably when he caught sight of me.

'Now where did you come from?' he giggled. He was one of those men who giggle a lot.

I always liked him.

Stoutening slightly and worried about it, he did extra punting to prevent obesity; he was a man who was for ever startlingly clean and tidy, which I admired, and he seldom sat down, even eating his breakfast standing. He never had a hair out of place. Alice was very short and slightly lame; she also was stout, and was ever kind. She was a woman who sewed most beautifully, and her sewing had great appeal for me. When she heard that I had played croquet as a girl she was plainly cheered at the thought.

We were given a large double room on the top floor, with a view of the lake, the swans, and those unbelievable rhododendrons. We booked in for the summer.

It was a most lovable house. It was full of memories, one felt them all the time. I daresay it could have had a ghost, or more than one of them. I always thought there was somebody there, but nothing worrying at all.

Being so near to Greenwich and Woolwich, there was quite a collection of young officers, and the place was gay. The Onslow and Lamorbey were such very different roofs, but what an amiable combination!

'I think we could do worse,' Robbie said, and that is a lot from him.

He could go up and down by train. He had come to a stage in his naval career when he was shortly due to serve five years overseas, and we knew that we could not take it. My headaches had become a menace, and it would be difficult for him to leave me alone like that. We had faced one of those shattering crises which come into people's lives, and which have to be met.

Robbie retired from the Navy in order to stay with me. I had felt horrible about it, for I had the idea that my health *had* been the factor to blame, and try as I would I could not find a doctor who could help me. It had been a momentous decision for him to have to make, and I owe my life to the fact that he did make it.

So we came that summer to Lamorbey, the house which was for many happy years our second home. Never ours, but always ours. What a beautiful place it was!

Lamorbey Park
Sidcup, Kent

Robbie's first retirement job was in the Admiralty in the department which dealt with obtaining jobs for retired N.O.s. I never felt that he enjoyed it very much, though he said little about it. A man's job is nothing to do with his wife, I felt that too, one has to leave it to him.

On arrival I found a huge bowl of flowers in my bedroom, and a dish of peaches from the garden. Bertie had ordered these. I was not too sure that this was a good idea, but Robbie said why worry? He likes peaches anyway.

The first night at a new hotel is always the acid test. We came down the long curling stairs and across the main hall into the panelled lounge, to the dining-room. This had been built on. The french windows opened on to a hedge of golden euonymus, which gave the impression of always being lit by the most radiant sunshine, a very happy thing. All our own vegetables were grown inside the walled back garden, and the chickens and ducks were reared in the grounds.

Afterwards we had coffee in the lounge, and then round came Bertie, all bright smile and twinkle eyes, looking for someone who would play snooker with him. Immediately he had been disposed of with people to play, along came Alice wanting to fix up some croquet, and I got wheedled into it. I was extremely worried about my prowess, for I had not had a mallet in my hands since the days at Whitchurch, and then I had been a child.

I was a very old child now! This, I told myself, is going to be my Waterloo and Alice won't ask me twice. I was wrong. I had to make a long shot three-quarters of the way down the lawn; I decided against shutting my eyes and having a swipe, hoping for the best. Nobody was more surprised than myself when I landed through the hoop.

That stroke put me on the map for the croquet list, fondly cherished by Alice, who adored a game, and from then on I had trouble. I wished to do at least two hours an evening on a book, which was my bread and butter, and I usually did this after dinner. But Alice was ever present. 'You can do that tomorrow, it's such a lovely evening', and all that sort of thing.

When the moon rose, and the heat of the day died, the games duty being done, Robbie and I would stroll round the silent golf-links together. I suppose it was the most romantic place in all the world for us, and frequently we return to walk there again, but not in the moonlight any more, alas.

There was the quiet loveliness of a peaceful roof over the head about Lamorbey, something of tall trees and velvet lawns. It was a house that had faded a little, discreet and dignified, with the magnolia scent I had learnt to love in Spain, and here we could be happy. The guests were just a big house party.

When Pip arrived back from Cirencester Agricultural College he was amazed to find what the place offered him. Its major advantage seemed to be the glorious faculty it possessed of offering an escape from parents if so desired. I could never be grateful enough that we had come here.

Lamorbey improved my actual English, and I never know how background can do this, but it can. Poona gave me plots, Cambridge Mansions encouraged the business side enormously and opened up new markets for me, but Lamorbey got me dead clear away from those sickening light romantic novels. Maybe the place taught me to think.

Three Cedars was the first book that I wrote there, the story of the three cedar trees which stood on the far side of the upper lake. I imagined that each in turn had been planted by a woman of the big house, who gave it her Christian name. Perhaps I had been working hard on improving my English and style for some years now, thanks to the devoted Robbie ('How do you spell "fuchsia"? No, that is *not* right'), and the time had come when I earned my reward. Anyway I always associated it with Lamorbey.

It was so gay.

I remember the summer's evening when I went round in the moonlight, kicked off my shoes and danced on the lawn for the sheer joy of being here. A startled hedgehog bundled himself off at speed. It was somehow the right thing to dance here. The house was fey, it made me fey-ish, too.

I particularly liked Bertie, though I knew he could be a danger spot. He could blow up into ghastly tempers when one flew for one's life. He could be quite generous with flowers and fruit, and was a man who was always amused at the gaieties of life, save for the sour moments of some hangover. He was, naturally, full of hangovers.

He had a private room at the back, and was for ever trying to persuade people to go there and drink with him. And oh, what Bertie could drink! Old Parr was his speciality. Now Robbie does not like whisky, being R.N. he is a gin man, and he wasn't that mad about Old Parr. I, being a lifelong teetotaller, was no good at all to Bertie in that line, but as I was a woman I had other advantages which I always felt he had marked down, and hoped—given luck—to do something about it. He wasn't going to get the luck, though he did not know it then. He was, of course, a devil with the girls.

Inmates led me into the rhododendrons and whispered frightful stories of this and that. 'And who do you think it was, my dear? I saw him coming down the stairs. It was *Bertie*!'

There was a lady who had the pet name of Sweetie who had had an affair, they said, with him, and often visited the place. Somehow or other Sweetie fitted into the pattern here, maybe because nobody was going to be such a fool as to quarrel with Bertie, and Bertie wandered round with her, all smiles and twinkles, picking huge bunches of flowers, baskets of fruit, and gathering a few dozen eggs, etc. There were moments when one travelled round the gardens and suddenly had to make a detour. 'Ssh! It's Bertie,' and there would be a couple spooning under a tree, or kissing beside the lake; one hurriedly fled without a sound.

His family were resentful, somewhat naturally, and everyone sympathised with them. We all felt sorry for dear little Alice, ever perplexed by what was going on, but with no clue as to how to stop it. I doubt if it could have been stopped, and said so.

'It's disgraceful,' said a more pious visitor.

'Oh, why worry? I had a father who was made that way, so perhaps I understand.'

'How disgusting!'

'Why? Life belongs to people to use it as they like. Bertie is none of our business. The thing to do is to keep quiet,' and I walked away.

But I had been well versed in the rectory at home in this tangled triangle of living, so maybe I had learnt that placidity is the only possible answer to it. My one certainty was that nothing I did would encourage him to have a go for me. He found me charming, complimentary at times, evasive at others. Thank heaven Bertie never caught up with me!

Cool trees, punting on the lake far into the night if one wished, sitting amongst the flowers and being awfully happy; what a place for scandals Lamorbey was! One night Bertie brought home with him a somewhat rowdy drunken friend of the nastiest nature and gave him dinner. It was plain that this man was out to pick a quarrel with someone, and he started it off with poor Captain Croker, who was the last man in the world for this sort of thing (and a darling!).

After dinner was done the men went out into the enclosed yard at the back of Lamorbey for a smoke and a chat. There it began, like a couple of schoolboys, and in the first swipe the rowdy visitor knocked off the Captain's glasses, so that he was powerless to defend himself. Another valiant man rushed in. Within a moment half the men who were staying there were milling in the back yard in a proper little-boy scrap.

My son came rushing back with the news.

'They're fighting in the yard.'

'Rubbish!' said Robbie, but went to see and in a moment there he was fighting bravely with the rest.

I'm afraid that I laughed.

Men never quite grow up, and as I know myself, when one starts a good fight one gets swept up with it and can't stop it. It goes on to glory—or the other thing—and our rowdy visitor got the other thing with a vengeance. He had to be taken up to a bathroom and bathed, and how that man bled!

It was then discovered—far too late—that he was an important somebody in Bertie's business, brought to dine with the directors and to be given V.I.P. reception. At all costs a good impression was to be made, and then this was what happened.

Finally he was restored and returned to Bertie's private sitting-room for lashings of Old Parr, and a general smoothing down.

I went for a walk by the lakes.

'This is an enchanting place to stay in,' I said.

Robbie was recovering somewhat from the fray in the back-yard. 'That's what *you* think!' said he grimly. He had cricked his neck.

On the very first night he had discovered that an old school friend from Dover College was resident there and they met like long-lost brothers. It always seems to be a little absurd to me that men who have shared the same scholastic education look upon it as being a bond, even more golden than the wedding ring. Now why?

I should never be carried away from my dancing-class days if some woman said to me, 'I was at Miss Crawford's with you.' My reply would possibly be, 'Oh, were you? Didn't you find Miss White a bit of a tartar?' But perhaps women don't feel about school in the same way.

Robbie's friend was musically minded and he played the piano divinely. At school he had not been too happy, owing to an unfortunate remark he had made about a dripping tap in the shower room. He said that the tap dripped in C sharp minor. You can imagine what a lot the little boys made of this. The man was probably quite right, and it was a remarkable simile, but it did not do much for him at school.

He had the best bedroom and in the grounds a remarkable beamed barn which he had lined with panelling, and where he did photography or played the piano when he felt like it. It was a most superb barn. He took beautiful photographs, and of course the old ladies of the place said they were sure that he photographed nudes there, though why they should think this, heaven only knows.

I always felt that he was rather an unhappy personality a little out of life, and one of those people who so longed to be in it to the top.

He made friends with the others, had never had a row in his life, and when Captain and Mrs. Brown came along he fell for her! Mrs. Brown was much younger than the Captain, who was so for God, for King and Country that it could hardly be true. I felt that she was unhappy too, for she always wandered about the grounds with a tiny gramophone she had, playing snatches from *Peer Gynt*.

One night when I could not sleep, and the moon was very high, I got the idea that something was going on, got up and went to the window. It would have been just before the dawn, the time when the whole world is so unbelievably beautiful, and here were Robbie's friend and Mrs. Brown coming back to the house from the barn. She was slender, gave you the idea of being rather boyish in a lanky sort of way. She had let down her hair, and it flew about her really very prettily, for she danced.

Robbie's school friend watched her, apparently adoring it. She looked like some pixie, from another world, and watching I felt her faun-like movements were something that could only happen in this place.

They were both so happy, and happiness is a very beautiful thing.

Next day when her pompous husband was having his breakfast—he always had three boiled eggs, which I thought was a bit much—I looked at him, and his wife. She was half asleep, rather forlorn, poor thing, a dim shadow of the joyously ebullient creature she had been last night. I wondered if *he* knew. Of course he didn't, and wasn't that all to the good?

Robbie has never been a jealous man, he gets amused and does nothing about it. He maintained that I must not be too offhand to Bertie in case he got annoyed (always a great possibility with Bertie), then we might have to leave this happy place.

'Keep him going,' said Robbie, with the optimism of one who does not appreciate the complications, 'and we'll sit pretty.'

'You mean *you* will?'

'Just keep Bertie going in a nice quiet way.'

'Keeping Bertie going in a nice quiet way' was *not simple*, for he was not a nice quiet man. I dreaded some inevitable muddle which would complicate everything.

In a way I placed Lamorbey with Gibraltar and Malta. Yet there was something of Whitchurch there, something of restful peace, time to enjoy oneself, to sit back and be leisurely.

I was at Lamorbey when I bought the car.

For some time I had wanted to do this, and one Christmas I persuaded poor Robbie to have driving lessons. I shall never know how he agreed, it was a dreadful experience for him, but he went through with it. I felt that a car would get us away from being always under a roof, and maybe this would be to the good. Driving would make such a difference to our lives, but I am, and always have been, hopeless at it.

I admit that I was surprised when Robbie gaily passed his test the first time, and I took him along to a dealer who was said to be an old friend, and we selected a car. It was second-hand; I had always had second-hands before, but if ever there was a dud, this was it. Our first venture in it was round Hyde Park, not so bad then as now, but after a few yards I rather wished that we could run into something, and end what was a nightmare of a drive. Ultimately I got out at the Achilles statue and said, 'I'll walk back to the Onslow, even if it kills me; for if that doesn't, driving with you most certainly will.'

He was hurt, but not angry.

We took this car down to Lamorbey with us, and what a terror it was! I did not know if it was Robbie's driving or the way the car reacted to it, or what it was. I took it out once myself in the grounds, hoping nobody would know, and I must say that I did find her very difficult to manage. Not that I can manage a car particularly well.

One day I got Robbie safely up to London to his job, then took the car out of the garage with considerable difficulty and up the hill into the small village (it *was* a village then, and a very sweet one). I hied myself to a garage.

In the main I have found strange garage people trying in the extreme. Unreliable and difficult, they would sell you a mad dog quite easily, and then say you were the one who drove it mad! They get away with anything. But this was a most charming man. He was never difficult, and always kind. I explained my dilemma, something was wrong here, it could be Robbie, it could be the car, what did I do about it? He asked if he could take the car just down the street on his own, and he did, bringing it safely back to where I waited. Then he said this was no car for a beginner. Robbie was new to driving, and he was trying out his 'prentice hand on a fairly rotten car, and he privately thought that whoever had sold it to us, friend or no friend, had seen us coming, and had done his worst by us.

That was the conclusion at which I had arrived quite a time previously.

In the garage was a brand-new Flying Standard, the car of that year. She had been a show car, and therefore was a little dusty, which meant that I could buy her well below the usual price. He said that he would allow me a good sum on the old

dud, which I still had with me because I could not get rid of it.
Would that fill the bill?

Awful uncertainty filled me, knowing that some gents who
run garages can be definitely non-gentlemen.

'You needn't pay it all down,' he said.

'That's not me,' I told him.

I decided that by slightly tightening the belt in another
direction I could do it, and I paid down a cheque on condition that
he would give Robbie lessons free if he needed them. He was enchanted with me. I then said, 'What about a little Morris for my son
at college?' for now I had met someone whom I could trust.

We got on fine.

I went home on the wings of a bird, with glee, and we hid
the new car in the garage, and he went back to put in the order
for a little Morris as a surprise for my son when he arrived for
his holidays. Nothing could have been better. I asked him to be
'really nice' to Robbie over the lessons, because N.O.s do not
take very well to being taught anything. He said that he understood this absolutely. Greenwich Naval College being so close,
he knew quite a lot about the behaviour of N.O.s.

'And,' said he, 'they are all the same, don't you worry, I
know; a white patch or gold leaves, it all works out the same
way. But you'll find that he'll like this.'

As the day wore on I became slightly alarmed about what
Robbie would say. I finished my work and walked down that
lovely tree-y walk to the station to meet him. There was the
sickly scent of sweet chestnuts in blossom, the faint whisper of
oaks, and the garlanded walls of the kitchen garden. Today
Lamorbey is a public park. Half the trees have gone, there has
been martyrdom of those glorious rhodies, and many people
who adored it have been homesick for it ever since. More get
the benefit of it, but in such a different way, and what has been
lost is irreplaceable. It can never be restored.

I met Robbie at the gate.

'Hello, whatever are you doing down here?' he asked, for I
did not often come as far.

With courage I said that I had come because I had something to tell him. I asked if he really liked the car that I had bought for him, and which had given me fits in Hyde Park. Yes, he said, he did! He thought that it was a very nice car. In horror, I said, but more timidly, did he not find it tricky to drive? He said no, he didn't. He was getting used to it. We saw the big mansion coming into sight between the trees, and perhaps the grey roof gave me courage.

'Something has happened,' I said.

'You didn't take her out yourself and have an accident in her?' he asked, almost fiercely.

'No, no, of course not,' and I told him this in the manner which suggested that such an adventure was quite impossible for me.

We did not go up to the house, but took the side door by the damson trees and went into the stable yard.

'I've got something here for you,' I said in a whisper, for now I was sick with fright lest he would be annoyed at the step which I had taken. There stood the black and green Flying Standard glorious in her newness, and sparkling in the sun of late afternoon in summer. She bore a number plate with EKE on it, and we always called her Little Eke. Robbie somehow *knew*. Perhaps my face gave me away.

'Oh, my God!' said Robbie, 'where the hell did you get that?'

'I found her,' I said with simplicity.

'She really is rather nice. Does she go?'

'Oh yes, beautifully, that was why I bought her, you see.'

'You bought her? Two cars?'

'Oh no, no, nothing like that. I swapped the old dud. The man says that he will show you how to drive her, and she is far simpler than that other awful thing.' I paused. 'It has all been paid for, don't worry, and you can't go back on it. Also I ordered a little Morris for Pip.'

Robbie eyed me severely. 'All I can say is that he must have been *some* garage man,' said he.

'He was very nice!'

'And I bet he *felt* very nice, too,' said Robbie.

He got into the car; he never gives himself away until he is sure (a strong trait in him), and then he said that he liked her. He just had time for a wash, a gin, and the nice man appeared ready to take him driving in her. After that he said that driving Little Eke was so simple that it couldn't be true.

She gave us several years of valiant service.

She made all the difference in the world to us, for now we could go away for week-ends in her, and could go far and wide, the sea whenever we wished it, and she really was delightful. I thanked heaven for the day when I took the law into my own hands and bought her.

We now had made this happy arrangement of the Onslow Court in winter, and Lamorbey always for the summer. Both had carefree atmospheres. Both left me free from the social side and the domestic chores, to do my work, and after that, enjoy myself. Lamorbey had the games influence, and although I hardly play them myself, I do find them interesting to watch.

The inhabitants were never as old as those at the Onslow Court. Lamorbey was overflowing with the young, and was the eternal inspiration for short stories. The lady and gentleman who danced in the moonlight, the young officer who de-bagged another young officer on Bexley Heath one joyful afternoon, coming back full of joyous abandon at the success of the venture, and then getting himself served with a writ. The young man's mother had got wild about it. She saw nothing funny in it at all, and now the young man had the jitters! It would *not* go well at Greenwich. It would not be considered so amusing by his own people, particularly if there was a fine attached. He had so little left. The purchase of a motor-bicycle had embarrassed him considerably and he was on the rocks.

One made a valiant attempt to comfort him (privately much amused that this had happened, but it was so much part of Lamorbey). What did it end in? Bertie came forward. He felt that young joys should be encouraged, and he would pay the fine. It was so like Bertie who when in an amiable mood was so

M

very amiable. I held his hand as a reward, and he sent me the best spray of orchids I had had for years.

'Now where did these come from?' asked Robbie, rather surprised.

'You?' I suggested.

'Good Lord, no! I don't do that sort of thing. It couldn't be Bertie?'

Bertie it was!

Of course, living in hotels all the time meant that I did far too much work, and I was irritated that I was able to work so much better out of my own home than in it, for a home is a liability in some ways; yet when you want a book from your reference library for research the hotel has you cold. I loved my own furniture, and missed it. Hotel furniture (even the nicest) is not the same thing, there is no history behind it. No hotel chest-of-drawers reminds you of Great-Grandmamma and such; I swing back to Victorian ancestry without a doubt, and maybe like all Victorians I am lost without a home.

Stupidly I kept telling myself, We *ought* to have a real home, with a door we shut on the outer world, and a garden in which we grow flowers, and all the little everydayness of four walls surrounding us, and a roof on top.

The feeling nagged at me, and one summer I made the idiotic mistake of getting a house in Oxted, in Surrey. At that time Oxted was a sort of inland Frinton, leastways that was how it looked the first time I saw it, and the house was pretty. It had red tiles and cream walls with beams on them, and a garden back and front.

It was a transitory move, that house with the fantail pigeons on the roof, and the chocolate box impression that it really was quite a good bet. Rose came down and helped me in. A couple of months later an emergency op moved me out of it at speed, and I was not sorry, for Oxted was more than I could bear. It was so dull.

I also found one detail for which I had not bargained.

Living the hotel life, I was accustomed to a crowd of acquaintances, people coming and going, always someone to talk to. Pip was back at college, Robbie away all day. Then people called on me, nice people, I am sure, kind people, and I returned their calls at the right hour and in the formal manner; and there it ended. I came to the conclusion that nobody had ever been de-bagged in Oxted. That there was nobody in the place half as nice as Bertie, and I had a yearning to see Carter again in the chocolate coat with the gold lace rings round the cuffs.

Had I outgrown the idea of a home? What a thought!

When I had finished my work in an hotel I went downstairs to recreations of all sorts, and a crowd of people to meet. In the home I worked at my writing, did the housework, knowing nobody really, and always returned to the desk.

I was thankful when I was whirled into a nursing home. 'Maybe we shall never have a home again,' I said to Rose, and privately I did not care.

'You just haven't got the right place,' she said happily enough. She was always right.

Maybe the real home would never have materialised at all save for a Sunday morning in spring, when Pip and I became bored with the Onslow Court and went out for a walk together. I have always found a stroll absorbing.

One of the delights of my earlier life had been to wander over empty houses. Prying, is what I suppose you would call it. I inherited this from my mother, who had never been known to pass by an empty house, but up the path she trotted, and if the doors were locked then she got inside in the more unladylike way, but see it she would. As far as she and I were concerned, the empty house offered us the greatest joy, and we would get as far as arranging where we would put our furniture in it, if . . .! There was intense accent on the 'if'.

'We could put the sideboard there,' Mother would say, 'but that leaves us at a bit of an impasse with the corner cupboard. Look, half the corners are round, how very odd! Now what *shall* we do about the corner cupboard?'

This was almost some sort of game that we played, and later

on we walked out again having settled everything to our satisfaction. It was quite harmless, and it amused us.

Just as when autumn came we took walks together in the grey twilight, hoping some neighbour had been kind enough to leave us an unveiled window with lights already lit. Then we could take a glimpse into somebody else's life, a peep into another world, for we loved houses. Mother always said that she got the bug from her own mother, who changed houses at such speed that the family could never keep up with her. Once she moved three times in one year. She also had another peculiar little trick of her own, for the minute she bought a house (and she must have bought dozens of them) she immediately had the doors re-hung the other way round. She had been known to block out a door, and put another somewhere else. Door-dotty, was what Mother said she was.

On this particular Sunday morning, in search of something to do, my son and I went sauntering down Pelham Street, not London's most interesting spot, crossed the Fulham Road, and then went on down Sloane Avenue. Proceeding gallantly we came to a new block of flats which had very recently been built, called Cranmer Court. The name got me. I have always been interested in the days of the eighth Henry and have written several books on them, and the thought of Cranmer wetted my whistle. Also, I had paid a visit to the block only three weeks previously. Dr. Spielman had given a party at the flat he had taken, one of the show flats, which, he told me, meant that it had three coats of paint to the other flats' two. A big help. These small details are a tremendous importance if you love a house. I had found that the flats employed the most polite porters I had ever met. I made further enquiries and learnt that they were Guardsmen, and whatever one may say, one can always tell a Guardsman but one can't tell him much. He knows.

Pip and I wandered round the corner into Whitehead's Grove, and he got the idea that it would be fun to get the key and have a look over the empty flat on the ground floor. Shades of Grandmamma and of my mother! Naturally I was not the sort of person to hold back, and we had nothing else to do. The letting office was actually open. There was quite the most charming girl in the office, I don't know if the company recognised her sterling value, but she would have let a flat to anyone. She had only three left, and when I asked if I could have the key she gave it to me.

'Maybe you'd like to go over it alone?' she said amiably, 'I always find it nicer that way myself.'

Off we went with the key.

We arrived at the block, the big doors swung open, and a Guardsman came to attention with a bang. There was black-and-white flooring, gracious chairs, and very attractive gilt mirrors on the walls. These caught my eye. The whole atmosphere of the place was what one would probably call 'superior', and there are times in life when it is very pleasant to be superior.

We went to the door of 150, and opened it on to home. For that was exactly what it was. Home with a capital H.

'I say, this is rather nice,' said Pip.

The hall might be ordinary, but the bedroom with its lovely cupboards had charm. Next door was the room I should dedicate to my writing, and here I was at Mother's game of arranging all my furniture in the place which I was seeing for the first time. The big double sitting-room with the fascinating glass doors was adorable. It looked out on to a charming garden of velvet-green lawns, with small cupressuses at the corners, very formal, but oh, how select!

The little kitchen had all the things I had never owned before, and was compact. I must say that both of us were enormously impressed by what we saw. Back we came into the double sitting-room. There was a radio niche in the wall.

'I shall keep goldfish in it,' I said.

'You'll take it?'

'If we can persuade Daddy.'

'We shall have to do something about Daddy,' he commented.

We went back with the key, talking it over, and I found the nice girl again, and we started to go into the matter. There was a restaurant in the building, also all the necessary shops, particularly a wine shop which perhaps my husband . . .?

'How right you are!' said I, 'he wouldn't give a hoot for the dairy, but the booze shop would enchant him.'

They had guest rooms if we wished to have guests to stay with us, not that I ever wanted guests to stay with me, for they demand too much and drive me mad; they had Hoovers on loan if ours got stuck up. They had in fact every mortal thing, including a private box-room for luggage, under the roof.

To me it looked rather as if someone had thought of everything here. I glanced at the nice girl, and because she seemed to be a very understanding person, I told her the truth.

'The bother is my husband!'

'You're not alone in that, possibly,' she said and smiled.

'No, but I've dropped several bricks over houses, and I think he might be dubious about taking another.'

'A flat is less trouble,' she suggested.

'Yes, I know.' Again I recalled Albert Bridge Road, and the brick that had turned out to be. Privately I had now returned to the phase when I was simply longing to get my furniture out of store, and enjoy living with it. It is, of course, the best way to work if only you can do it. I explained the awful difficulty in getting domestic help. The nice girl agreed to this, and in fact the flat had no room for a 'liver-inner'. They were, she thought, dead as the dodo. There were lots of daily women in the neighbourhood though, for there were huge blocks of dwellings round the corner, and she had yet to meet the person who had difficulty in this way. I knew that she was speaking the truth. She thought that a flat was much easier to run than a house, and that there would be no trouble.

I looked dubiously at her.

I said, 'Now what I want to do is to entice my husband round here this afternoon, but it has to be done with tact. He won't know what he is coming to see.'

'Quite,' said the girl. Then she told me that I was not alone in this, for crowds of women did exactly the same thing, bringing their unsuspecting husbands round for a look-see, and going away having taken the flat. 'This afternoon,' said she.

That was a rather sticky lunch at the Onslow Court with Robbie, for we felt we had a guilty secret up our sleeves, and then we went for a walk to take the air. What about having a look at Chelsea? we suggested, so down Pelham Street we went yet again, and along Sloane Avenue into Cranmer Court.

'Look at those nice new flats!' said I.

'Hideous!' said he. It was hardly a propitious start to the work in hand. He is far too fond of the unpruned word; he never uses two when one will do, and what a one for the flat which I was wanting to take for myself! We walked him round to the dead blank windows of number 150 which we had seen this morning. 'What fun to go inside and have a peep!' I said.

Plainly I realised that Robbie could see no fun in this at all, but he is one of those patiently kind men who will do anything to keep the family quiet, and even suffer himself for them. Pip went round to the office to get the key, and we waited. His attention was now arrested by the ex-Guardsman on duty. 'Smart,' was what he said.

But when we got inside the flat Robbie loved it.

There was always a particular atmosphere about number 150, maybe because there was no dweller on the threshold, for when you live in a honeycomb the dweller ceases to be. The place was too new for him, anyway. The rooms attracted one by their prettiness, even Robbie recognised this, for the flat exuded happiness in some strange way.

'How do you feel about it? We *could* take it,' I said as calmly as I could force myself to speak.

He was more than slightly surprised. For one second he gave me that gimlet look which he always gave to sailors, it was what Pip and I knew as the aye-aye-sir look. Then, in a strained voice he said, 'I suppose you have taken it already?'

I am truthful. 'Not quite, but almost,' I explained.

'We want no more mistakes. The Albert Bridge Road, Oxted, and all that.'

'I know, but this *is* a workable proposition and the others were not. Then we could not manage without a living-in maid, and times being so awkward it was impossible to get one. This is halfway between the hotel and the home of our own.'

We went closely into details. I went back and asked Dr. Spielman about any difficulties, and he said that he had not found any, and he was one of the first residents in the block. We found we could take it from Michaelmas Day, and we did. Then we should be returning from Lamorbey to a new phase in our lives. I went through the utter joy of arranging a peach and lime sitting-room, and an apricot bedroom with deep navy-blue curtains. The writing-room would be green, for this is a restful colour to work with, the bathroom scarlet and white.

Off we went to Lamorbey for the summer. Here in the acres of lovely grounds, punting on the lake, listening to a gramophone playing, I was not worried. We could, at a pinch, always return to the Onslow Court–Lamorbey life if we wished.

All through that summer I came up to town in Little Eke to have a peep to see how the men were getting on decorating the flat. It looked quite beautiful. On Michaelmas Day we would move in.

Late one night I sat by the upper lake, with the smell of roses everywhere, and about me the superb peace of night in summer. Pip and Robbie were with me.

'It's going to be all right this time,' Pip said, for he has some of my feelings about dwellers on thresholds, and some houses wishing you well, and others most certainly not doing so.

On the lawn they were playing moonlight croquet. It was one of Alice's ultra-energetic evenings. Bertie had worn the lot out with snooker, and now had retired with the men to Old Parr in his private room. I'll miss this place, I thought. But I never really left it (until the day it was taken from me, to my bitter regret), and we would go back there from time to time.

'Lamorbey will still be here,' Robbie said, 'also Christmases at the Onslow Court. Nothing will stop that.'

We had not thought of a war, then.

150 Cranmer Court
Chelsea, SW3

How pretty the flat looked the night we moved in, with supper
in the restaurant! There were peach organdi curtains I had made
at Lamorbey, for someone had nobly lent me a sewing machine.
I had had difficulty with the eighteen-foot pelmet I had to make,
and solved this in the end by dangling it out of the window, and
gallantly machined away. Suddenly I heard a shriek from the
bedroom below. The poor lady had been lying down, feeling
slightly poorly, and looking up had seen a big wriggling
'animal', was what she said, coming down over her window. It
was my pelmet!

The furniture came out of store from Messrs. Ebbutt's at
Croydon, who had served my father-in-law and grandfather-
in-law, it seemed, and there is nothing like keeping a good move
in the family. When the war came they moved me in and out
at speed. I always said that the furniture got to know them, and
said, 'Home, John,' as it got into their vans.

In the hall of number 150 I had arranged the polar bear rug
which I had bought in a crazy moment on a Norwegian glacier.
A polar bear is a wonderful thing to have in a brand-new hall,
and oh, how *distingué*!

I had had some demur about the blue bedroom, which was
devised to match the new bedspread which I had made for
Robbie, and which had the whole of his naval career on it. I

must say there had been a good deal more of his naval career than I had ever expected when I began the sewing.

The bedroom looked charming now that it was done, and the only difficulty which it provided was that of Tommy, the cat from the fish shop, who always climbed in at night and lay down on my bed for a snooze, waking me with the most appalling stench of fish I have ever known. There were other complications, I admit, for one summer's night Adrian Conan Doyle's pet python had got out from his house in The Gateways over the way. It is a little surprising when people come and ask if by chance you have seen a meandering python about the place.

A little daily maid arrived in time for breakfast from Battersea, and never in her whole time with me was she late. That first night I realised that the flat had something which had not been provided anywhere else, it was the ease of running it. It was possible to shut the door on it, and go away, and there were porters and people who guarded it. I don't think it ever occurred to me that it could be burgled, and it never was. When I came to Cranmer Court—which is a small village of its own—I never realised that I should spend so many many years of my life here, and probably die here.

It was unbelievably well run.

Mr. Vaughan was our head porter. He appeared in person late in the afternoon of the move-in. He times his appearance with infinite discretion. There he was with the best salute in the world, and the most dignified manner.

'Anything we can do for you, madam?' and when I said, 'Nothing at all,' a little taken aback, 'I trust you find your own porter efficient, madam; his name is Cook.'

'He's a miracle. God's gift.'

'If in any trouble, madam, you have only to ring on the house telephone and I shall be here.' He indicated the house telephone which hitherto I had not observed. 'I am the head porter, my name is Vaughan, and we wish you to be satisfied with the flat.'

Satisfied! I should think I was!

Of course after that it was too obvious that everything would run on oiled wheels, and with the kind attentions of dear Cook and our Mr. Vaughan heaven was very near. Though naturally I should never dare to ring up Mr. Vaughan, how could I?

Later when the war came he became a colonel in the Commandos, training them in Scotland. Efficiency was his second name. At eight each morning he trotted out a squad of porters to come on duty, after the manner of Buckingham Palace. In winter a lantern came along with them. What a handsome upright lot they were, falling into step just behind one, coming to attention on the instant, and how polished were those salutes! (Game and set to George Taylor, ex-Coldstreams, still with us.)

But how can I ever live up to it all? I asked myself.

I had had a look into the porter's room at the door of each block of flats, and there was a long list of rules hung up, and they *were* rules! Porters must walk two paces behind the residents, and no resident must be permitted to carry a parcel. Hints on proper behaviour, the length of hair, the shine on boots, and so on, hints which today you could not give, but in the thirties you did, and Mr. Vaughan was standing for no nonsense.

Early on I ran into trouble with him and was to find that although I was a tenant, I was there to be rebuked if I did the wrong thing. No liberties, please. I am one of those rather ridiculous and wildly clean people, which I think he appreciated. My curtains were changed every fortnight, and my goodness, living in London asks that of you. My window-sills gleamed whiter than white even at a time before the detergent had come into general use.

Mr. Vaughan wished to see me, and I went to the door. 'The window-sills, madam,' said he.

I was proud of my window-sills, and so I was not abashed. 'I wash them myself,' I said with glowing confidence, which I ought to know is always a mistake.

'This is appreciated, madam,' but oh dear! The hawk-like eye was on me, he obviously hadn't been a sergeant-major for nothing. Here we go! I told myself, and I was right. 'You use a detergent of some kind?' I did. 'It is a matter of our paint,' said he. 'Soap and water, madam, *if* you please. Nothing stronger, or it ruins the paint, and it costs money to do it again.'

'Soap and water does not do it as well,' I maintained, with some spark of fight still left in me.

'Elbow grease is an assistant, madam.'

How I admired him for it! I went back into the flat and had a good laugh, but of course the man had got something there and he *was* in the right.

One day I came home from a trip into the country, and opening my front door saw that the hall was knee-deep in soap suds. What on earth was my polar bear doing under all that horror?

'Oh, my goodness!' I gasped.

Cook rushed up, came to speedy attention and saluted magnificently, then said to himself, 'Blimey,' which hardly seemed to go with the rest.

With that nose for news which all journalists (including myself) reserve with pride, Mr. Vaughan appeared out of the distance. One glance at our hall told him exactly what had happened. Detergents had begun to arrive, and apparently the flat above mine had been having a joyful day with them. The drains did not like them, and not taking them too well hiccoughed up the lot into my flat. The gents' cloaks had overflowed. Mr. Vaughan knew exactly what to do. I think he always would, for later when I had been shattered by a land mine he again knew exactly what to do. On Judgment Day I hope to meet him in the queue, for I am sure that he will tell me the ropes, bless him.

'One moment, madam,' said he. 'You sit in the car for ten minutes only, and then the flat will be entirely satisfactory for your use. Leave this to us.'

I wanted to stay and help, but oh no, that could *not* be permitted. I realised then that one did not say no. I was wafted back into the car with more salutes, the door firmly shut on me, and ten minutes later (to the tick) a Guardsman came to attention and saluted with the words, 'I have to inform you, madam, that your flat is now satisfactory.'

My flat was entirely satisfactory. It was just as I had originally left it, and the polar bear had not lost a single whisker.

Later I discovered that Mr. Vaughan was attached to the Beefeaters. I found it out when there were photos in the paper of what Robbie would have called 'a bit of a do' at Buckingham Palace. The Beefeaters were on duty there, and one of them looked very like our Mr. Vaughan. I was not mistaken in this, for it *was* our Mr. Vaughan.

'Oh, yes, madam,' said my porter gravely. 'Mr. Vaughan is most certainly a Beefeater.'

I thought, Next time he does it I must see him drive away in his regalia, for I have never come face to face with a full-blown Beefeater. But Mr. Vaughan was very particular about it when he was in the 'rig of the day'. I even went to the Palace gates to await their arrival, but in they came in a covered wagon of some sort, and in through the gates before one realised they were there. Inside they sat in two rows, like the old-time carrier's cart, and travelled face to face.

I never saw him in the rig of the day.

If I had been dubious about coming to Cranmer Court to live, then I had been wrong. The flat brought me such luck, and I gave joyous parties in it. I got a job with Hugh Cudlipp on the *Sunday Pictorial*, the editorship of the beauty page on *Woman's Own*, and everything went swimmingly.

I suppose the answer really is that in the writing career one is eternally building up. I had never wished to be one of those dazzling young writers who burst into Fleet Street in a blaze of glory with a first novel and then are never heard of again. I wanted more. Now I was on radio a lot. Val Gielgud was being very kind to me with plays, I have every reason to be deeply grateful to him, for plays are my magnet. This is what I want most of all.

'It's a lucky flat,' I told Robbie, and he too thought so.

I tried to enquire into its history and found it was built on ground which once had been part of Chelsea Common. That was at the period when the little street now known as Whitehead's Grove had contained one big mansion and some cottages, in whose gardens lilies-of-the-valley grew wild. They had come down and The Gateways had gone up in their place, very attractive little houses for those who wanted a *pied-à-terre* and not a lot of work entailing servants.

Once a circus had come to this part of the world and had set up its Big Top here. I always hoped that it was somewhere near where my flat stood. How enchanting it would be if I found the place pleasantly haunted by red-nosed Joeys, and coquettish ballerinas, the tight-rope walkers, and the merry acrobats! But of course that did not happen. These things come and go and I always mourn the fact that the Cremorne Gardens went, for although people tell me that Battersea Fun Fair is exactly like them, that is not true. The Cremorne was class—a forbidden word, of course, but it meant a lot then. In 1850 my great-aunt wrote home to her mamma from her hotel in Argyll Square about the Cremorne:

> Last night was so enjoyable at the Cremorne Gardens. The rose bowers were enchanting, such music and such laughter! The gentlemen were rogueish, most amusing, surely there has never been anywhere so pleasant as the Cremorne? It must live for ever. We drove home exhausted, and the sky was just brightening for the new day.
>
> Mary Bloom

Those were the real Chelsea days, and I always smile when I think of the enjoyment my great-aunts got there. But change comes to all of us, we all have our day. And what a ghastly thought it is that this goes for me also!

The moment the war came, Robbie's job took him away and I had to get out. I had just renewed my lease, and that was an expensive venture. The furniture disappeared in one of Mr. Ebbutt's vans, and there I was sitting in Little Eke, clasping a large tank of Japanese tri-tails in my arms, and destined for Buckinghamshire.

It was an irony to be there only ten days, as Robbie was transferred back to London, and we went once more to the Onslow Court. Dear Miss Willatt had gone, and that I hated. I stayed there just long enough for the war to arrive in London itself, and to spend night after night in the air-raid shelter.

By the advanced autumn, Robbie again working in London, I managed to get a furnished flat back in Cranmer Court (number 82) with the idea of holding on to this until the moment when I could take an unfurnished one. In January I was offered number 226, which was at the far end of White-head's Grove, and a big flat. Up came the furniture and we got it in. 'If we're going to die, let's die together,' I told Great-Aunt Minnie's bureau.

That was the spring when the vigorous bombing increased, and there was that awful night when we were plainly in the front line. I know I sat in the corridor almost hoping that I should be hit and get it over. They say you never know the moment when you are going to be hit, I certainly did not, but a land mine came into the back where the velvet lawns spread, and those sweet little cupressuses went for six. When I came to, a roof was on top of me, and four walls had enormous holes in them, through which I could see a great deal going on outside.

'Just look at this!' I said to Robbie, indicating the mêlée about me.

Funny things happen to the homeless, I know. One lives in bleak hotels, getting in where one can, and ultimately I spent quite a time down at Letchworth, where my doctor's family were staying, and he most kindly got me a room. I was there for months, and although they were pleasant and at times I was very happy there, nobody likes being evacuated. We should be here for ever, was what I felt.

Another horror came to me. An ex-love of mine was leaving his house there, we both thought the war would go on for years, and he offered me the house, which I bought. I saw it on a summer's afternoon, with a lot of roses out, and an attractive pool in the garden. These things mislead a woman. I wanted a place of my own again. How keen is the longing for home at times, and alas how dangerous it can be!

Gernon Elms was another Fantails (which I had called the Oxted house). It was quite the coldest house in England, and unworkable. I had thought there was every chance of getting somebody to help me, someone with a child perhaps, but it did not work out. I got back to Cranmer Court again. It meant moments of flight, when the agonising flying bombs came, but I did keep a foothold here for the rest of the war.

Just before the end I returned to number 48 where I was then living. I awaited peace day there. I could write in Cranmer Court, which had been much more difficult in other places, I had friends here, and I could work the home. But a flat is never a home in the same way, I suppose, though I am still here, years on. A flat is a resting place. It makes few demands, but it also gives back little return in deep feelings. It has not the subtle emotions of a house. I shall leave nothing behind me here, and the woman who comes after me will never even know that once I was happy here. A house can provide that knowledge, but a flat cannot.

Maybe the answer lies in the fact that, although I do not know it, I am not really looking for a roof and four walls. I need somewhere to sleep and eat, to do my work and at times to entertain my friends. The flat stays background, it never dominates me as houses can, but it never turns out to be a first-class pest.

Maybe my love and longing for Fleet Street has overtaken me in some strange way of its own. There is no roof to Fleet Street. Up above it is the bare sky, the clouds, a lot of them, the stars—too few! I love the clutter of untidy offices, the noise of the moving presses, and the friends one runs into from time to time, and whom I adore.

When you come to think of it, perhaps Fleet Street itself is my real home.